T0334539

"Insights from one of the leading researchers working at the intersection of music, psychology, and computer science."

        –**Dan Levitin**, *author of* This Is Your Brain on Music

"A graceful and precise introduction into the intricacy of what ordinary humans manage to learn about music, naturally and automatically, just by listening."

        –**Gary Marcus**, *author of* Guitar Zero

"Honing demonstrates that ordinary listeners, whether children or adults, are a lot more musically savvy than they think they are."

        –**Sandra Trehub**, *Department of Psychology, University of Toronto*

MUSIC COGNITION

THE BASICS

Why do people attach importance to the wordless language we call music? *Music Cognition: The Basics* considers the role of our cognitive functions, such as perception, memory, attention, and expectation in perceiving, making, and appreciating music.

In this volume, Henkjan Honing explores the active role these functions play in how music makes us feel; exhilarated, soothed, or inspired. Grounded in the latest research in areas of psychology, biology, and cognitive neuroscience, and with clear examples throughout, this book concentrates on underappreciated musical skills such as sense of rhythm, beat induction, and relative pitch, that make people intrinsically musical creatures—supporting the conviction that all humans have a unique, instinctive attraction to music.

The scope of the topics discussed ranges from the ability of newborns to perceive a beat, to the unexpected musical expertise of ordinary listeners. It is a must read for anyone studying the psychology of music, auditory perception, or simply interested in why we enjoy music the way we do.

Henkjan Honing is professor of Music Cognition at both the Faculty of Humanities and Faculty of Science at the University of Amsterdam and member elect of the Royal Netherlands Academy of Arts and Sciences.

The Basics

The Basics is a highly successful series of accessible guidebooks which provide an overview of the fundamental principles of a subject area in a jargon-free and undaunting format.

Intended for students approaching a subject for the first time, the books both introduce the essentials of a subject and provide an ideal springboard for further study. With over 50 titles spanning subjects from artificial intelligence (AI) to women's studies, *The Basics* are an ideal starting point for students seeking to understand a subject area.

Each text comes with recommendations for further study and gradually introduces the complexities and nuances within a subject.

For a full list of titles in this series, please visit www.routledge.com/The-Basics/book-series/B

MUSIC COGNITION

THE BASICS

Henkjan Honing

LONDON AND NEW YORK

First published 2022
by Routledge
2 Park Square, Milton Park, Abingdon, Oxon OX14 4RN

and by Routledge
605 Third Avenue, New York, NY 10158

Routledge is an imprint of the Taylor & Francis Group, an informa business

British Library Cataloguing-in-Publication Data
A catalogue record for this book is available from the British Library

Library of Congress Cataloging-in-Publication Data
Library of Congress Control Number: 2021936940

ISBN: 978-0-367-74526-4 (hbk)
ISBN: 978-0-367-74500-4 (pbk)
ISBN: 978-1-003-15830-1 (ebk)

DOI: 10.4324/9781003158301

Typeset in Bembo
by Taylor & Francis Books

For my nieces and nephews.

CONTENTS

FIGURES

BOXES

PREFACE

When you talk with people about musicality, you often get reactions like "Oh, but I'm not musical at all" or "I'm hopeless at keeping a tune." But if you pursue the matter, it turns out most of these people often listen to music with the greatest of pleasure. Why is it people have such a low opinion of themselves when it comes to their own musicality?

This book will show how listeners are more musical than they think. Music plays with our hearing, our memory, our emotions, and our expectations in a fascinating way. But as listeners we're often unaware of the fact that we ourselves play an active role in making music exhilarating, soothing, and inspiring. In reality, the listening doesn't happen in the outer world of audible sound but in the inner world of our minds and brains.

In this book, I will use recent research results to show that we are all musical creatures, whether we are talking about the sense of rhythm in newborn babies, the ability of toddlers to keep the beat, or the unforeseen musical expertise of ordinary listeners.

Admittedly, these are relatively novel results—most were published in scientific journals in the last two decades—but they all support the growing conviction among researchers that we all share a predisposition for music.

I would like to thank the editorial staff at Routledge for their enthusiasm and support in realizing this adapted and fully revised edition of *Musical Cognition* (Routledge, 2014). I thank Henk ter Borg, Pieter de Bruijn Kops, and Ed' Korlaar of Nieuw Amsterdam Uitgevers for their contributions to the original Dutch publication, Sherry MacDonald for drafting parts of the English translation, and

Anne-Marie Vervelde for her help in realizing the current Routledge Basics edition.

As for the research, I am particularly grateful to the Netherlands Organisation for Scientific Research (NWO), the Royal Netherlands Academy of Arts and Sciences (KNAW), and several European Framework Programmes (e.g., FP5, FP6), all of which helped facilitate my research during the past thirty years. I hope to continue to benefit from their resources in the future.

And lastly, most of the ideas brought together in this book are not new. They build on the insights of the pioneers who gave shape to the discipline of music cognition. I cannot name them all here, but I have tried to mention them in the text itself or in the references. I thank all of them for their shoulders and, indirectly, for lending me their ears.

INTRODUCTION
WHAT THIS BOOK IS ABOUT

Why do people attach such importance to the wordless language we call music? Many a philosopher has agonized over this question. The answer this book proposes is that music is not a language but a game: music as beneficial play. In music, our cognitive functions, such as observation, memory, attention, and expectation, are stimulated, as in a mating ritual with the listener but without need and without danger and in a way that we find pleasurable, instructive, soothing, and exciting.

I will attempt to chart this mating ritual. I will not always succeed, because we do not yet know enough about the role of music or musicality in human cognitive-emotional development. But, thanks to recent research results in the fields of psychology and the cognitive sciences, I will be able to be less speculative about the subject than many of my predecessors.

This book also differs from earlier publications on music cognition in that psycho-physiological and neurological jargon will be avoided wherever possible. Nor are there are any illustrations of the ear or diagrams of how the ear works. Instead, the focus will be on what happens inside a person's brain, between the ears, since, as a subsequent chapter will reveal, acoustics are less relevant to this.

There will also be no pictures of the brain, despite its being indisputably located between the ears. This is because discussions of the role of memory, attention, perception, and expectation in listening to music are possible without having to visualize the specific locations where these functions are directed.

Lastly, this book will not contain any fragments of sheet music: this would give the "experts" an advantage over the "laymen," which would be entirely contrary to my intentions. All diagrams used are meant to be intelligible to everyone.

As such, this book aims to be a gentle introduction into the intricacies of what we all manage to learn about music, naturally and spontaneously, just by listening.

PART 1

DE DO DO DO, DE DA DA DA: THE TONE OF SPEECH AND MUSIC

FIRST LISTENING EXPERIENCES

Why do babies like infant-directed speech better than normal speech? Are we born musical? What do we know about the capacity for music and music cognition?

On the face of it, it is a strange phenomenon: adults who, the moment they lean over to peer into a baby buggy, start babbling a curious baby talk. And it doesn't just happen to fathers and mothers; it overcomes many people in the same situation. In fact, we all seem to be capable of it, this "de do do do, de da da da."

But what exactly are we saying to our little fellow human beings? What message can be derived from this "de do do do, de da da da?"

The technical term for this baby talk is *infant-directed speech* (IDS). It is a form of speech that distinguishes itself from normal adult speech through its higher overall pitch, exaggerated melodic contours, slower tempo, and greater rhythmic variation. It appears to be a kind of musical language; however, it is one with an indistinct meaning and virtually no grammar. For these reasons, I will call it "musical prosody." Babies love it, and coo with delight in response to the rhythmic little melodies, which often have the same charm as pop songs like The Police's "De do do do, de da da da" and Kylie Minogue's hit "La la la."

Numerous sound archives around the world have recordings of these musical conversations between adults and children. If you listen to several of them, most of the time you won't be able to understand what's being said, but you will be able to identify the situation and particularly the mood because of the tone. It will quickly become apparent whether the message is playful,

DOI: 10.4324/9781003158301-2

instructive, or admonitory. Words of encouragement, such as
"That's the way!" or "Well done!" are usually uttered in an
ascending and subsequently descending tone, with the emphasis on
the highest point of the melody. Warnings such as "No, stop it!"
or "Be careful, don't touch!" on the other hand, are generally
voiced at a slightly lower pitch, with a short, staccato-like rhythm.
If the speech were to be filtered out so that its sounds or phonemes
were no longer audible and only the music remained, it would still
be clear whether encouragement or warning was involved. This is
because the relevant information is contained more in the melody
and rhythm than it is in the words themselves.

Most linguists see the use of rhythm, dynamics, and intonation
as an aid for making infants familiar with the words and sentence
structures of the language of the culture in which they will be raised.
Words and word divisions are emphasized through exaggerated
intonation contours and varied rhythmic intervals, thereby facilitating
the process of learning a specific language.

From a developmental perspective, the period during which
parents use IDS is remarkably long. Infants have a distinct preference
for IDS from the moment they are born, only developing an interest
in adult speech after about nine months. Before that time, they
appear to listen mostly to the (musical) sounds themselves. An
interest in specific words, word division, and sound structure only
comes after about a year, at which time they also begin to utter their
first meaningful words. The characterization of IDS as an aid to
learning specific languages, therefore, seems less plausible to me, at
least with respect to the earliest months of our lifespan.

An alternative might be to see the sensitivity to IDS not as a
preparation for speech but as a form of communication in its own
right: a kind of "musical prosody" used to communicate and
discover the world for as long as "real" speech is absent.

If you subsequently emphasize the type of information most
commonly conveyed in those aspects of speech in which infants
have the greatest interest during their first nine months, the
conclusion must be that IDS is, first and foremost, a way of con-
veying emotional information. It is an emotional language that,
even without grammar, is still meaningful. The role of melody
and rhythm in this emotional language is as significant as the role
of word order is insignificant. This is because during their first

year, infants are primarily interested in the musical aspects of babbling. Both caregivers and infants make use of the melodic, rhythmic, and dynamic aspects of IDS; they speak the same "language"—the "language of emotion."

In 2009 the scientific journal *Current Biology* published an empirical study with the intriguing conclusion that French babies cry differently than German babies. Recordings made by the researchers demonstrated convincingly that German newborns generally cry with a descending pitch contour; French newborns, on the other hand, with an ascending pitch contour, descending slightly only at the end. This was a surprising observation, particularly in light of the commonly accepted theory that when one cries, the pitch contour will always descend as a physiological consequence of the decreasing pressure during the production of sound. Apparently, though, babies only a few days old can influence not only the volume and dynamic contour, but also the pitch contour of their crying. Why would they do this?

The researchers interpreted these differences as the first steps in the development of language: in spoken French, the average intonation contour is ascending, while in German it is just the opposite. Knowing that human hearing is already functional during the last trimester of pregnancy led the researchers to conclude that these babies absorbed the intonation patterns of the spoken language in their environment during the last months of pregnancy and consequently imitated it when they cried. This observation was also surprising because until then it was generally assumed that infants only develop an awareness for their mother tongue between six and eighteen months, at the age they start babbling and learning their parents' language. Could this indeed be unique evidence, as the researchers emphasized, that language sensitivity is already present at a very early stage, or could it be an indication of something entirely different?

MUSICALITY PRECEDES LANGUAGE

While the facts appear to be clear and convincing, this interpretation is a typical example of what one could call a language bias: the linguist's understandable enthusiasm to interpret many phenomena in the world as linguistic. In this case, however, I believe it is a misjudgement. There is much more to suggest that these newborn babies exhibit an aptitude whose origins are found not in language but in music.

At the beginning of this chapter, we saw that babies possess a keen perceptual sensitivity for the melodic, rhythmic, and dynamic aspects of sound, aspects that linguists are inclined to categorize under the term "prosody," but which are in fact the building blocks of music. Only much later in a child's development does he make use of this "musical prosody," for instance in recognizing word boundaries. But these very early indications of musical aptitude are in essence nonlinguistic. It is a matter of "illiterate listening": a human ability to discern, interpret, and appreciate musical nuances already from day one, long before the baby has uttered, let alone conceived, a single word. It is the preverbal stage that is dominated by musical listening.

It will therefore come as no surprise that the musical components of IDS also form an important part of speech later in life, although by then of course, we use rhythm, stress, and intonation infinitely more subtly than when talking to infants. From the tone of someone's utterance, we can decipher whether he or she is happy, angry, or excited. *C'est le ton qui fait la musique*, it's not what you say but how you say it. And we usually have little difficulty in deciding whether what is said is a question, an assertion, or an ironic remark.

But there are also other reasons for viewing IDS as an early sign of musical behaviour rather than as a preparation for adult speech. The relationship between the *linguistic* aspects of IDS (such as the meaning of words) and the *musical* aspects (such as rhythm and melody) is clearly visible, especially in those cultures where the native language is a tonal one, such as Mandarin Chinese. In tonal languages, a melody can easily conflict with the meaning of the word, which is determined by pitch. A well-known example is the word "ma" in Mandarin Chinese. Depending on the pitch at which it is uttered, it can mean either "mother" or "horse." It is striking that in such cases the emotional information of IDS "wins" over the purely phonemic aspects. During the earliest months, the musical information of a word is thus much more important than its specific meaning.

Canadian developmental psychologist Laurel J. Trainor has been conducting extensive research in this area. She is not alone in believing that the most important function of IDS is to create and maintain an emotional relationship between the caregiver and the infant. She has shown in various studies that young infants have no difficulty at all in deciphering the emotional information in speech or in a children's song at the moment it's sung. It is very exciting when you realize that infants can derive specific emotional information from the complex timing, phrasing, and variations in pitch in the language their parents speak with them: minimal differences in pitch, intonation, and length of syllables, corresponding to emotions ranging from "comfort" to "fear" and "surprise" to "affection," are interpreted correctly. Striking, too, is the fact that infants can distinguish these "melodious" emotions before they are able to recognize them in facial expressions. The cognitive functions involved in listening to music and speech appear to precede the development of visual perception. (In some ways, a head start would seem logical because babies already have functional hearing some three months before they are born.)

It appears that many of the musical skills we normally attribute to adults are also present in infants from the age of a few days to several months. Four-month-old babies can distinguish pitch intervals with great precision, as well as remember and recognize simple folksongs. Infants also seem to be much more sensitive to a wide range of subtle melodic and rhythmic differences than most adults. A study conducted at the University of Miami, in which both adults and six-month-old infants listened to melodies from Western and Javanese musical traditions, bears this out. Javanese melodies sound distinctly different to Western ears: the tones are tuned differently, have different frequency ratios (i.e., pitch intervals) than they do in our culture. In the listening experiment, one tone in each melody was tuned either slightly higher or slightly lower than normal. The adult listeners were easily able to identify these changes in the Western melodies, but not in the Javanese variations. The (North American) infants, on the other hand, could hear the differences in both the Western and the Javanese melodies.

All these studies support the idea that we're born with a set of listening skills but can lose our sensitivity to specific musical nuances as we become accustomed to the conventions of the musical tradition in which we grow up. In the case of the Miami study, this means that the more deeply people in the West become embedded in prevailing music traditions, the less they are able to distinguish tonal nuances in the less frequently heard Javanese music.

The phenomenon of the loss of certain sensitivities relevant to our perception of music is paralleled in our linguistic development. Here, too, certain tonal nuances will often no longer be noticed or precisely reproducible at a later age. A case in point is the ability to hear the difference between an "r" and an "l." Japanese infants can hear the difference with no difficulty at all, while Japanese adults struggle to make the distinction. In fact, humans lose flexibility in exchange for a more efficient processing of those aspects that are relevant to a specific language or musical tradition.

This kind of developmental psychology research has also been conducted on other aspects of music, such as rhythm and timing, with similar results. Infants and young children turn out to be extremely sensitive to melodic and rhythmic differences in speech and music, and often have a more highly developed sensitivity in these areas than the average adult. The flexibility of young children in experiencing and interpreting music disappears by about the time they start to go to school. By this age they will have been heavily influenced by culture-specific aspects of music such as tonal and harmonic structure. Such aspects are clearly learned as a result of exposure to the musical patterns characteristic of the music of the culture in which they are raised.

In short, the ability to recognize subtle differences in rhythm and pitch—in both speech and music—appears to be innate. From a young age we are very skilled decoders of the often emotionally laden, nonlinguistic information embedded in the musical prosody—the rhythm, stress, and intonation—of both music and speech. Language, with its specific word order and virtually unlimited lexicon and multiplicity of meanings, only blossoms much later in human beings. Therefore tells us something about the function of music in human development and the innateness of musicality to each individual. So how important is all this? Apart from the essential significance of musical prosody for emotional bonding between infants and parents, what is the *evolutionary advantage* of music and musicality?[1]

MUSIC AND EVOLUTION

In the evolutionary sense, music can be described as "pointless": it does not quell our hunger, nor do we seem to live a day longer because of it. In fact, music appears to be of little use to us, aside perhaps from the pleasure that creating or listening to it affords us. This, at least, is what cognitive psychologist Steven Pinker maintains. At the end of the 1990s, he famously characterized music as "auditory cheesecake": a delightful dessert but, from an evolutionary perspective, no more than a by-product of language (see Box 1.1).

Pinker provoked considerable anger in many music scholars at the time by contrasting language with music, and citing language as an example of evolutionary relevance and music as an example of evolutionary irrelevance. But might Pinker be right in this? Are there any arguments to show that music may have played a definitive role in man's evolutionary development? Might music not be an "adaptation" after all, one that has contributed to the survival of man as a species? Or is music, as he suggests, no more than a pleasant side effect of more important functions like speech and language? Not an adaptation, but an "exaptation," in which existing traits are put to new use (as an example: feathers originally served as insulation, but later, via gliding, were selected as an effective means of locomotion)?

Music scholars—and music educators in particular—took offence at Pinker's ideas and have since put a great deal of effort into searching for scientific evidence to show that music does count (note that Pinker did *not* state that music does not matter, but that our capacity for music is probably not an adaptation). The so-called "Mozart effect" is the best-known result of this quest to show the relevance and importance of music. Psychologist Frances H. Rauscher demonstrated that students performed noticeably better on IQ tests after listening to a Mozart sonata. In the experiment, about forty students were divided into groups and exposed for ten minutes to either Mozart (Sonata for two pianos in D major, K448), relaxation instructions, or silence. Students that had listened to Mozart did better on an IQ-related spatial task than the members of the other two groups. At last, scientific evidence demonstrating the importance of music: it makes us smarter! Or so it seemed.

In subsequent years, new experiments showed that the effect was attributable not so much to the music itself as to the positive mood induced in the listeners *as a result of* listening to the music. Canadian music psychologist E. Glenn Schellenberg showed that, in addition to the Mozart effect, there is also a Schubert effect, a Sibelius effect, and even a Blur effect. And lo and behold: listening to "your kind" of music does (for about ten minutes) improve your spatial skills! But, to the extent that your mood is improved, the same effect could also be achieved when you hear an interesting story or eat a banana.

Not the music itself, but the mood created by the music (being happy and alert) is what influences the scores on the IQ tests. Though this indirect relationship may be a disappointment to Mozart fans, it does highlight an important effect of music: it can heavily influence or reinforce your mood. Music is a very good mood enhancer or regulator. It is actually one of the most mentioned reasons why people listen to music. But the question remains: why? It is quite possible that our early experiences with IDS have something to do with it. Recent neurological research is producing increasing evidence showing that music not only stimulates the production of the "feel-good" *endorphins* as well as "rewarding" *dopamines* (both neurotransmitters: chemical messengers of the brain), but also influences the way the brain develops or repairs itself after brain damage. These are aspects of music that are central in recent neurobiological research on our *capacity for music* (see under Further reading).

As for the Mozart effect and the commotion around it: it is, of course, an admission of weakness to demonstrate the importance of music by showing that it positively influences another human characteristic, above all, one we appear to consider more important, namely, intelligence. In fact, this just confirms the notion that music is a second-class activity. But even if it was a central activity in our current lives, this does not mean it would prove Pinker wrong, in the sense that the capacity for music also played a central role in human evolution.

Presumably, the evolutionary biologist Charles Darwin (1809–1882) would have disagreed with Pinker; as he would with the famous psychologist William James (1842–1910), who qualified music as a by-product of the hearing organ. More than anything, Darwin believed that music was a great mystery: "As neither the enjoyment nor the capacity of producing musical notes are faculties of the least use to man ... they must be ranked amongst the most mysterious with which he is endowed." But Darwin also proposed that music was most likely a product of "sexual selection," comparable to a bird's flaunting of an impressive display of seductive feathers (see Box 1.1). Evolutionary psychologist Geoffrey F. Miller recently expanded on Darwin's idea. Arguing that the sex appeal of pop stars supports Darwin's principle of sexual selection, Miller offers Jimi Hendrix and his countless groupies as a primary example. He also sees the important role pop music plays in adolescence as "proof" of Darwin's idea: in his view, music (and the other art forms) is the medium through which we reveal our mental and cognitive skills to others and are able to judge those same skills in others. And all of this, for the sake of the advancement of sexual selection. This sounds convincing, were it not for the fact that major differences could then be expected in the anatomy and behaviour of men and women, as is the case where sexual selection in songbirds is concerned. However, unlike with songbirds, whales, frogs, and other "song"-producing creatures, there is no substantial difference in the way men or women perceive or produce music nor in their physiology related to music processing. We all know from first-hand experience the important role that is played by music in adolescence, that period of intense development in terms of identity and sexuality. But this hardly constitutes proof that music is a result of sexual selection. Numerous counter examples of pop stars with noticeably less sex appeal than Jimi Hendrix spring to mind. Moreover, on average, rock and pop stars turn out to die twice as young. It is like the brazen sheep that lure the ewes away from the dominant male: they, too, die younger. This is also why the more patient rams, which live longer, are ultimately more successful in reproduction. In this sense, the assumed role of music in sexual selection is a hypothesis which, like so many evolutionarily motivated hypotheses, is more readily voiced than it is empirically supported.

Whatever the *biological origins of music*, music does of course play an important role in our cultural and social life, from ceremonies and rituals involving dance and song to seeking and reinforcing our identities from adolescence into adulthood. Just think of the pop stars who capture the fascination of entire football stadiums, or the effect that carefully chosen pop songs have on American presidential campaigns: "High Hopes" by Frank Sinatra on John F. Kennedy's, "Born in the USA" by Bruce Springsteen on George Bush Jr.'s, or "Better Way" by Ben Harper on Barack Obama's. According to some authors, the most important function of music is to enhance the social cohesion of the group. Music is the "social glue" that keeps the group together and promotes cooperation, thus strengthening the group feeling. One such author is the historian William H. McNeill. He sees an essential role for music in the "blurring of self-awareness and the heightening of fellow-feeling." In his view, this function derives from the prehistoric singing and dancing around the campfire in preparation for the hunt, when music contributed indirectly to the survival of the group. It is difficult to refute this other than by invoking the dilemma of the chicken or the egg. Does music not require many of the same cognitive skills that contribute to social processes?

Evolutionary psychologist Robin Dunbar has convincingly linked this activity to the phenomenon of gossiping in language, which he calls "vocal grooming" (grooming being chimpanzees' favourite pastime). In the same way, music can be seen as "musical grooming," as an effective means of achieving social cohesion by promoting the bond between parent and child (just like IDS) or between people in general, think for instance of the effect that music has on large crowds in a stadium.

All these hypotheses suggest that music might have a biological origin and served some evolutionary gain (See Further reading). But next to a biological basis, music has many more purposes, as we shall see shortly. Like sex, music too surely fulfils more functions than just that of the strict survival of the group (see Box 1.1).

MUSIC PLAYS WITH THE LISTENER

Pinker was probably right when he wrote: "I suspect music is auditory cheesecake, an exquisite confection crafted to tickle the sensitive spots of … our mental faculties." Or, to express his idea in more technical terms: music affects our brains at specific places, thereby stimulating the production of unique substances that have a pleasurable effect on our mood. Rather than a by-product of evolution, it could well be a characteristic that survived natural selection in order to stimulate and develop our mental faculties. As such, our capacity for music is seen as an *exaptation*, that surfaced by chance without having been specifically selected, and shifted its function during evolution. Once it existed, however, it was further perfected through natural (or sexual) selection and passed on as such to future generations. Pinker's idea may actually be a very fruitful hypothesis whose significance has wrongfully gone unacknowledged because of all the criticism it elicited. After all, the purely evolutionary explanations for the origins of music mentioned earlier largely overlook the *experience* of music we all share: the pleasure we derive from it, not only from the acrobatics of making it but also from the act of listening to it. Nearly everyone listens to music and appreciates it. But music also *plays* with the listener; it is neither threatening nor indispensable. Normally we like that; it helps us to explore the world and handle our emotions so that we're fully prepared for when it really counts.

As such, play is a phenomenon where nature and culture come together. From that perspective, play is not only an exploration of and preparation for the real thing—think of the young lion cubs learning how to fight through play in order to be able to hunt prey better later in life—but also a relatively innocuous activity that especially generates a lot of fun.

At the very least, play has four important characteristics. In the first place, it is not threatening; in this sense, it appears to be outside everyday reality. An example might be the short Internet film in which a team of hitched-up huskies are lying about somewhere near the North Pole waiting for their next ride. Suddenly a few polar bears come into view. Completely unexpectedly, the huskies aren't attacked. Instead, one polar bear responds to the playful bowing of one of the dogs and ends up in a position of full surrender—on the ground with his feet in the air. A surprising turn of events: a natural threat becomes innocent play.

Secondly, though not serious in itself, "play" is taken seriously. In his famous book *Homo Ludens* ("Man the Player"), Dutch historian Johan Huizinga (1872–1945) offers the disarming example of the little boy sitting at the front of a row of chairs pretending he's the engine of a train. When his father tries to hug him, the boy says: "Don't kiss the engine, Daddy, or the carriages won't think it's real." Play is meant to be taken as seriously as possible—that much we know "by nature."

Thirdly, there's the pleasure in play, such as the hedonistic pleasure in listening, as Pinker labels it; play as something you can completely surrender to and that can afford you pleasure, enjoyment, and new insights.

And, lastly, there's the challenge of play. It doesn't necessarily have to be pleasurable; it can also challenge and even thwart you. It is precisely the friction between what we know and what we're capable of, our cognitive skills, and the new possibilities that can be explored or experienced through play that leads to new experiences. Thus, "Bossa Nova" and "Bossa Electrica" will suddenly sound very different if you happen to listen to the classical Brazilian sambas on which this popular music is based first.

This is why, in addition to describing the significance of music in evolutionary terms—having the direct function of influencing our mood and the indirect function of creating social bonds—I would especially like to characterize music as stimulating play *for* and *with* our mental functions. The idea of music as "playing with the listener" emphasizes the fact that music, like any well-played game, should be taken seriously.

In listening, we experiment freely (albeit often unconsciously) with our mental functions. It is a kind of delayed seriousness about life, the delayed maturity so characteristic of human beings in comparison with other species. At the same time, when listening we are also exploring the mental functions of others as hidden in the expressions of *their* play, music.

As a final example: we are all experts in regulating our mood through music. If we want to reinforce our upbeat and light-hearted mood, we know precisely which music to choose from our collection (without always appreciating the fact that our neighbours may be in quite a different mood). When we are sad, we know exactly how to intensify that mood, or rather, to wallow in it: we play that music or that song. At yet another moment, we simply put on something intended to dispel our sadness or sense of loss, like an antidote. Listening to music can therefore be a form of exercising our emotions. On the one hand, it is a kind of mood regulator without pills; it can intensify or weaken our mood. On the other, it can help us prepare ourselves for the real emotional experience so that when the time comes, the experience itself will be a bit less daunting.

BOX 1.1   THEORIES ABOUT THE ORIGINS OF MUSICALITY

Theories about the origins of musicality can be classified in three kinds:

1   *Adaptationist accounts suggesting reproductive benefits.* Evolutionary biologist Charles Darwin thought music was primarily a result of the evolutionary process of *sexual selection*, music-making as an effective way to impress potential partners.
2   *Adaptationist accounts suggesting survival benefits.* Evolutionary psychologist Robin Dunbar and others suggested that music's main function might be to improve and increase *social bonding*, strong social bonds being crucial in the survival of our human predecessors.
3   *Nonadaptationist accounts.* Well-known example is the "auditory cheesecake" idea of evolutionary psychologist Steven Pinker, suggesting music to be a pleasurable by-product of adaptations that evolved for *other* functions than music. But note that, recently, theories have been proposed that try to combine these theories (see Further reading).

SUMMARY

As adults we tend to communicate with newborns in a more musical than linguistic way. Our vocal "de do do do, de da da da" is called "infant-directed speech" (IDS). In this language of emotion, the role of melody and rhythm is more significant than the words themselves. Minimal differences in pitch, intonation, and length of syllables correspond to emotions ranging from "comfort" to "fear" and "surprise" to "affection". We are born with a set of musical skills that allows us to detect and express emotions. However, sometimes we can lose our sensitivity to particular musical nuances as we become accustomed to the conventions of the musical tradition in which we grow up.

NOTE

1   For now, I will use the terms "music" and "musicality" rather loosely and interchangeably, and define them more precisely in Chapter 6.

FURTHER READING

Honing, H. (2018). "Musicality as an upbeat to music: Introduction and research agenda." In H. Honing (Ed.), *The Origins of Musicality* (pp. 3–20). Cambridge, MA: MIT Press.

Levitin, D. J. (2019). *This Is Your Brain on Music: Understanding a Human Obsession*. New York, NY: Penguin.

Savage, P., Loui, P., Tarr, B., Schachner, A., Glowacki, L., Mithen, S., & Fitch, W. (2021). "Music as a coevolved system for social bonding." *Behavioral and Brain Sciences*, 1–36.

Trehub, S. E., Weiss, M. W., & Cirelli, L. K. (2019). "Musicality across the lifespan." In P. J. Rentfrow & D. J. Levitin (Eds.), *Foundations in Music Psychology: Theory and Research* (pp. 265–303). Cambridge, MA: The MIT Press.

THE ILLITERATE LISTENER

Why is superficial listening considered harmful? "Easy" Abba versus "Great" Bach? What do music philosophers think? Should we turn music theory on its ear?

Before moving on to discuss the "ordinary" listener, I would first like to consider the "professional" listener, the music critic who regularly reports on his listening experiences for newspapers and magazines.

It is quite exceptional to be asked to put your response to music into words for the benefit of others: to be able to write, for example, that musical notes "escaped through the secret sound holes midway the Allegretto, into a fanciful garden in a godforsaken suburb of an imaginary Paris," or that the musician played "as if a tree trunk were being swept along on the wildly churning then suddenly gently rippling water of some unfathomable river."

What is striking about these and other quotations from concert reviews is the metaphorical language used by the critics. Might this be because a *direct* description of the listening experience is problematic or perhaps even fundamentally impossible?

Despite these doubts, music critics have a wealth of music-technical terms at their disposal with which to make clear to the reader the nature of the underlying musical structure, from "compound meters" and "polyrhythms" to "tone clusters" and "tone series." Some of these terms will evoke memories of our music lessons in secondary school, in which, along with music notation and music history, a music-related vocabulary often formed part of the curriculum.

Being able to describe or put into words a musical experience is still seen by many as an exceptional skill, demonstrating both

DOI: 10.4324/9781003158301-3

musical knowledge and insight. To say that music is "beautiful," "cool," or "invigorates you while you're studying" isn't enough; the same things can be said in any context. When music professionals hear such formulations they often shake their wise heads despondently; the essential aspects of the composition appear to have escaped the listener. The underlying reasoning is that because the layman can't refer to those aspects, he probably also can't *hear* them. At best, he can reveal something about how the music affected his mood: it moved him, gave him pleasure, or made him sad or excited.

But is it true that the layman therefore misses the essential aspects of the composition? Does most of the impact of the music escape the illiterate listener, who doesn't have a wealth of music-technical terms at his disposal or a talent for metaphorical language? Does he really not hear the music? Or does the listening *remain* superficial because the illiterate listener only listens to "easy" music—from Abba to the Backstreet Boys—and not to the "true" Great Music?

In his plea for Great Listening ("*Het Grote Luisteren*"), a denunciation of our culture's "superficial listening," Dutch music critic Elmer Schönberger appears to be suggesting the latter. He makes a distinction between Western classical music—the Great Music—on the one hand, and pop, jazz, and world music on the other, maintaining that those who don't listen to Great Music run the risk of missing out on Great Listening.

Though his indictment is undoubtedly a well-meant attempt to attract more listeners to Western classical music, it also bears witness to a rather unabashedly proclaimed elitism. It is not for nothing that he writes: "Mine is a call to snobbism."

Schönberger is not alone in his elitism. Several years ago, conductor and pianist Daniel Barenboim also launched an attack on what he called "superficial listening." In his second BBC Reith Lecture (from 2006), titled "The Neglected Sense," he focused on what he saw, certainly in comparison to the eye, as the neglected ear of today's youth. He also complained about the ubiquitous muzak at supermarkets and airports, the lack of attention for Great Music, and the general loss of the skill of listening.

In short, irritation with the role music plays in our daily lives concerns quite a few music professionals. The refrain is familiar: Barenboim and Schönberger are only two of a long succession of complainers about the alleged vulgarization of our society and the superficial listening of the younger generation for whom Western classical music plays only a limited role. Both authors belong to a generation shaped by German music sociologist Theodor W. Adorno (1902–1969), who argued that the culture industry, with its "vulgarized derivatives," makes people passive and compliant and, worse still, denies, and ultimately destroys, thinking.

But things haven't turned out quite so badly. In fact, it is my contention that the fear of the "superficial listener" is entirely unfounded.

SUPERFICIAL LISTENING

One should seriously question the claim that young "illiterate" listeners listen superficially. While it might be true that they lack a lot of explicit knowledge about music, does this also mean they cannot *experience* music, in the same way as one might say that an illiterate person cannot enjoy a book?

With respect to music, I believe the opposite is true: the impact of music is strongest precisely when the listener is young and illiterate. All but a few musicians will have had a powerful, emotionally charged musical experience during their adolescence that was decisive for the role music later came to play in their lives, a (life-changing) experience that probably still forms a source of inspiration.

The British music psychologist John Sloboda, who has done extensive research on music and musical expertise and on the role of emotions in both, has demonstrated that repeated exposure to emotionally charged music during adolescence plays a crucial role in the development of musical "top talent." In fact, a powerful listening experience at a young age usually guarantees a successful musical development later.

So, the notion of superficial listening among the young is mistaken: receptivity to music is at its peak in the young listener. The Dutch critic Schönberger longs for the time when he, too, was an illiterate listener, a sixteen-year-old who played the same record over and over again, "each time waiting endlessly for the wonder of that one chord, that one modulation, that one rest." Or, as Dutch philosopher and publicist Ger Groot put it in his review of Schönberger's columns published in *Het Gebroken Oor* ("The Broken Ear"): a young listener who "knows of such heights that disdain for the lesser becomes irrelevant."

However, it is not my goal here to idealize the direct, unstructured, pure experience. While that experience may be intense, research on implicit learning reveals that it is more difficult to generalize and integrate it with other knowledge. This may also be why it is difficult to put it into words. The more familiar you become with a certain genre of music, the more order and structure you hear in it—and that will influence and possibly change the experience of listening to it.

From the cognitive perspective, several things can also be said about how putting an experience into words can influence the nature of that experience. A study from the visual domain, for example, demonstrates how having words for different colours influences the ability to see those colours. If two slightly differently coloured surfaces are assessed in terms of color difference and both are called "green," fewer differences will be noticed than if one is called "green" and the other "blue." This is a good example of how the availability of a word—a linguistic category resulting from knowledge—can influence perception. The same is true of music. "Knowing about music," having access to more categories in which to divide musical phenomena, has a distinct effect on the way music is heard and experienced. In my view, though, the role of expertise and explicit musical knowledge is often overstated and the differences between music experts and young inexperienced listeners are not, as I will show later, as great as might be expected.

In summary—and by way of unsolicited advice to the music educators among or around you—I therefore propose that extra attention be paid to *listening*, especially at the primary school level. It may be that children listen to so-called "superficial music," but why not also expose them in a playful way to other kinds of music? And if children do "listen superficially," why not help them discover all the things that can be heard in "their" music?

Of course, this approach differs little from one that many music teachers are already pursuing. My main concern is that a better balance be found between listening to music and putting the experience of music into words. Music teaching can be less linguistic; it can use fewer words and symbols to help interpret and understand the music.

Music comprises not only an abstract, architectural composition but also, and in equal measure, nuances of meaning and emotional information conveyed through its execution. This is why we prefer one performance to another; the same notes may be played in a different, unique way, but the performance *practice*, together with the impact it has on the listening experience, is in principle nonlinguistic and inexpressible.

This is also why, even though in the case of most classical and pop music you know exactly what's coming, some passages of a musical composition will continue to surprise you. In music theory textbooks, it is either difficult or impossible to find the terms that capture that enduring sensation in words. Conversely, a person may know what label to apply to which rhythm (for example, *syncopation*), but this says nothing about the pleasure of listening to rhythmic music. An exciting rhythm can be heard and appreciated, but repeating the experience in words still appears to be impossible.

From the scientific perspective, there is quite a bit that can be said about the listener's experience. That experience can largely be understood through methods like the ones used in the study on color and taste nuances. Most people may not be able to *describe* the difference between two flavours, but they can *taste* it. It is no different with listening: though we may not know exactly why a specific turn in the music moves us so deeply, there is no doubt that we *hear* it.

In short, a specific knowledge of music is not a prerequisite for being musical; in fact, knowledge about music and listening to music have relatively little in common. Compare this with the theory part of a driving test: while it provides structure to reality and meaningful links between traffic signs, it says nothing about the actual experience of driving a car, which is, after all, what it's all about for everyone who's taking a driving test.

SUMMARY

While illiterate listeners lack the knowledge of professional musicians or musicologists, they are not less able to listen to and appreciate music. They often experience music in a way not dissimilar from professional musicians. The impact of music might be strongest when listeners are young and illiterate. Research shows that repeated exposure to emotionally charged music during adolescence plays a crucial role in the development of musical "top talent". Therefore, primary and secondary schools should pay attention to listening to "superficial" as well as other kinds of music, and help children to discover aspects that might not, or might as well, be heard in their favorite music.

FURTHER READING

Adorno, T. W. (2001). "On the fetish character in music and the regression of listening." In J. M. Bernstein (Ed.), *The Culture Industry: Selected Essays on Mass Culture*. New York: Routledge.

Bamberger, J. (1991). *The Mind Behind the Musical Ear: How Children Develop Musical Intelligence*. Cambridge, Mass.: Harvard University Press.

Levitin, D. J. (2012). "What does it mean to be musical?" *Neuron*, 73 (4), 633–637.

PART 2

OOH-OOH-OOH:
THE MAGIC OF MUSIC

MUSIC AS MYSTERY

How come music research is not always about science? Is it possible to find objective methods to measure subjective experiences, like listening to music? Would a scientific understanding of music take away the mystery?

Everyone who has a liking for music occasionally wonders what defines that affinity. What makes some music so cheerful and other music so sombre? Why do certain melodies stick in our mind? Why is one pianist's timing so unique?

Answering these and similar questions is the essence of musicology—or so you would think. In reality, it has been a long time since scientific theories about the perception, appreciation, and practice of music topped the research agenda of musicologists. More precisely, this has not been the case since Austrian musicologist Guido Adler (1855–1941) divided the field into historical musicology and systematic musicology in the 19th century. He placed the study of the laws of music, until then the focal point of the discipline, in the systematic musicology subdiscipline. In later years, the focus of musicology shifted increasingly to cultural, cultural-historical, and repertoire-related research.

More recently, this shift has been further reinforced with the advent of postmodernism, a movement within the humanities that sees little value in the objective methods of the social and natural sciences and that seriously questions the purpose and need of studying laws and patterns. There may at times be good reasons for this approach, even in musicology. But, broadly speaking, I believe the "new" musicology has become stuck in a sceptical approach that, from the outset, has excluded every opportunity for the scientific study of music and the listening experience.

DOI: 10.4324/9781003158301-5

To claim that because a musical experience is subjective and personal and *feels* unique it cannot be studied objectively, is a "classical" misperception. In fact, the methods and techniques of cognitive science, which focus especially on mental processes, are perfectly suited to helping expand our understanding of music perception and of the listening process and the listening experience.

It is, of course, understandable that musicians and musicologists embrace the notions of individual expression and their subjective impressions. Subjectivity is a fundamental prerequisite to making music; it is the essence of the musical art form, in which the unique, the personal, plays a key role. Searching for similarities, patterns, and structure is not the first thing you think of as you rock inconsolably to the *Adagietto* from Mahler's Fifth, or sing along tearfully with Dolly Parton.

The very *idea* that patterns or rules may be formulated that could explain all that beauty would be enough to arouse considerable suspicion in many people. Just imagine if the secret of music were to be revealed; the mystery of and fascination with it would disappear instantly. And that, for musicians and music researchers alike, is the very worst thing that could happen.

If you ask people what they see as the mysterious or magical in music, it turns out to be not the notes in the score but the *performance*—the specific interpretation of the music and the reaction to that performance—coupled with the listening experience. The slightest change of tone in an aria or delay in the playing of a guitar chord can be profoundly moving: we all have examples of this. The emotional response can even be so overwhelming it can impede the grasping or "understanding" of the performance at hand, because it is often the inexpressible nuances of a performance that make it so impressive. Just as it is often the "little things […] that [can] ruin everything" (Dostoyevsky, 1866).

Reasoning along these lines, it becomes a question for the philosophy of science: *is it even possible* to understand listening and the listening experience? Many music philosophers have agonized over this question. And the answer, after endless peregrinations, is usually a simple "no."

But are we making it too difficult for ourselves? Perhaps music is not a mystery at all. At least, no more of a mystery than language or other human activities such as playing chess, or a sport, or making love; all phenomena that science has been able to decipher successfully. Or should music be approached as an exceptional form of structured sound with all kinds of psychophysical characteristics that can teach us something about our listening experience?

Why go to all this trouble? The answer is because the study of music—the parsing, analysing, interpreting of the smaller parts of a complex and ostensibly incomprehensible whole—ultimately make this beautiful human phenomenon even more beautiful and more intriguing, just as our admiration for the human body grows, as brain and MRI scans allow us to observe exactly "how it all works." With this in mind, I believe there are no appreciable risks in the scientific study—empirical and formal—of the music-listening experience. Methods borrowed from, for example, psychology and computer science, lend themselves well for mapping out the different aspects of music and music listening.

Before we broach this subject in more detail, though, I would first like to describe two alternative visions of music: "music as language" and "music as sound." These will be discussed in the next two chapters.

BOX 3.1 STUDY OF MUSIC IN THE 19TH CENTURY

Guido Adler (1855–1942) divided the study of music into three subfields:

1   *Systematic musicology* refers to those disciplines of musicology that explore the foundations of music from different points of view, such as acoustics, physiology, psychology, anthropology, music theory, sociology, and aesthetics. But note that, while systematic musicology may have seemed to be an extension to musicology in the late 19th century (according to Adler), one could argue that it is the original musicology, and one that is central in current music research (see Further reading).
2   *Historical musicology* studies music from a historical point of view. In theory, "music history" could refer to the study of the history of any type or genre of music (e.g., the history of Indian music or the history of rock).
3   *Music theory* is the study of the practices and possibilities of music, often concerned with describing how musicians and composers make music, including tuning systems and composition methods among other topics.

SUMMARY

During most of the 20th century theories about the perception, production, and appreciation of music were mostly absent in the research agenda of musicologists. Since music appreciation is a highly individual experience it would simply be too subjective to be researched. This is a classical misperception; as is the fear that knowledge would take away the mystery. In fact, the scientific study of music—analysing the smaller parts of a complex and ostensibly incomprehensive whole—ultimately makes this beautiful phenomenon even more beautiful and intriguing.

FURTHER READING

Honing, H. (2006). "On the growing role of observation, formalization and experimental method in musicology." *Empirical Musicological Review*, 1, 2–5.

Jacoby, N., Margulis, E. H., Clayton, M., Hannon, E., Honing, H., Iversen, J., […] Wald-Fuhrmann, M. (2020). "Cross-cultural work in music cognition: Challenges, insights and recommendations." *Music Perception*, 37 (3), 185–195.

Parncutt, R. (2007). "Systematic musicology and the history and future of western musical scholarship." *Journal of Interdisciplinary Music Studies*, 1 (1), 1–32.

4

MUSIC AS LANGUAGE

Is music a universal language? How did Noam Chomsky's revolutionary ideas inspire comparisons between language and music? Can we experience music by reading a musical score? Do music and language have a common origin?

Language and music have a lot in common. In addition to diverse structural aspects, like the ordering of distinct elements (words, notes) into a larger whole, they share a communicative function and are both unique human phenomena. As is so often said, music is a language, or even, music is a universal language, a language that transcends all language barriers. But is this true, or is it simply an exaggeration?

Music and language are usually compared at the level of syntax: music is divided into notes and phrases, language into words and sentences. This presupposes an analogy between language and music that has inspired many music researchers to use methods from linguistics to analyse music.

A well-known example is composer and conductor Leonard Bernstein (1918–1990), who gave a series of popular lectures on the subject at Harvard University in 1973. At the time, Bernstein was highly impressed by the ideas of computational linguist Noam Chomsky. Around 1965, Chomsky had caused a veritable revolution in linguistics by compellingly demonstrating that every language could be characterized as a set of identical, innate rules (a *universal grammar*), which are applied by every language-user to a group of specific words varying from language to language (the *lexicon*) in order to transform those recognizable linguistic utterances (sentences); hence the label "transformational generative grammar."

In his book *The Unanswered Question* (a transcription of the televised version of the Harvard lectures), Bernstein writes how he

DOI: 10.4324/9781003158301-6

was euphoric for more than a year about the implications of what he calls the "Chomsky Connection," namely, the potential relationships between the (innate) grammar of language and that of music. In his Harvard lectures, he made an analogy between notes and phonemes, phrases and words, and musical sections and sentences. He also set the now legendary sample sentences from linguistics—"John loves Mary" and "Mary is loved by John"—to music.

But this assumed parallel between language and music was quickly disproven. The surface structure (*syntax*) of language can vary considerably, as is the case in the two examples above, while the meaning (*semantics*) can remain the same. Chomsky's theory clearly demonstrated this by showing how sentences with distinct surface forms can be identical in their deep structures.

Applying these insights to music was doomed to fail because the notion of semantics, as it is used in linguistics, is absent in music. While language can easily refer to an object or concept, this plays no role of significance in music. In fact, this is one of the most important differences—if not *the* most important difference— between language and music.

But Bernstein wasn't the only enthusiast. Music theorist Fred Lerdahl and linguist Ray Jackendoff joined forces in 1983 to publish their *A Generative Theory of Tonal Music*. In their book, the authors set out to explicitly define the music-theoretical knowledge a listener implicitly uses when listening to music. They devised a (semi-)formal theory that describes the musical intuitions of a listener who possesses significant experience in the Western classical idiom. In that sense it was one of the first cognitive theories about music.

The illustration below (Figure 4.1) graphically depicts an example of such a structural analysis in simplified form. The melodic relationships between the notes are rendered in a reverse tree structure, with the "leaves" of the tree, the notes, at the bottom (take note that this melody—"Shave and a haircut"—will return in Chapter 9).

In such structural analyses, the elements have a hierarchical relationship: some elements—in this case the notes or groups of notes—are secondary to others. In a melodic analysis, for example, the notes essential to the melody are distinguished from those that are "merely" decorative. An analysis of the phrasing structure looks

Figure 4.1 Structural analysis of a familiar melody.

at those notes that "belong" together and the way they are grouped in phrases and sub-phrases. A temporal analysis examines which notes are metrically important and which are not.

In Figure 4.1, for example, the last note (C) is secondary to the first note (C) because it hangs on a lateral branch. The third note (G) is the lowest in the hierarchy and therefore the least important. In short, the fewer the number of branches between a leaf (a note) and the "trunk" (at the top of the illustration), the greater the importance of that note in terms of the analysis.

Syntactical tree structures like these are derived from Chomsky's transformational generative linguistics, where they are used to visualize the grammatical structure of sentences, like in the illustration below (Figure 4.2).

In a linguistic tree, the branches are named or labelled, for instance with an "S" for "sentence," an "NP" for "noun phrase," and an "N" for "noun." These labels are used to determine which branches are and are not possible, so as to eliminate, at least in some

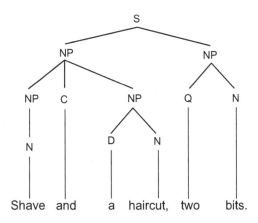

Figure 4.2 Example of a linguistic tree.

languages, the possibility that an adjective is placed after a noun instead of before it.

Music has considerably fewer grammatical restrictions than language; notes and phrases can be used in any number of combinations and sequences. This does not mean that structure plays no role at all in music, but one cannot, in music, say that a structure is syntactically wrong based on the semantic categories (NP, V, C) that underpin syntactic categories in language. "Mary loved is John by" is possible in music, but not in spoken or written language meant to communicate something. In this sense, music is closer to poetry, where the laws of syntax play a lesser role. But some researchers, for whom the language–music analogy remains too alluring, continue the search for structural similarities. Even in recent studies that resist the Chomskyan research agenda, the tree structure remains a key concept intended to facilitate reasoning about language, music, and visual information along similar lines.

The same can be said of Lerdahl and Jackendoff's theory, although (despite their claim) their diagrams should not be interpreted as a grammar. Rather, they are a graphical representation of a set of preference rules that show how the listener both interprets individual notes and constructs a unified whole out of their melodic, harmonic, and metric structures.

Several questions play a role in the formulation of these preference rules. Which aspects of music strike the listener most when he or she listens to it? Which draw the most attention and which play a supporting role? In a stream of notes, which phrases does the listener hear, and how are they ordered in relation to each other? Based on which musical information does the listener assign a certain time signature to the music?

The aim of Lerdahl and Jackendoff's theory was to make explicit the music-theoretical knowledge that the listener implicitly has at his disposal when listening. With their theory, which envisages a listener with extensive listening experience in a specific musical idiom, the authors sought to offer a formal description of the listener's musical intuitions.

Naturally, Lerdahl and Jackendoff's music-theoretical model also met with criticism. One criticism being that much of the analysis was left to the reader's interpretation; For example, the way in which formal preference rules should be combined to attain a factual music theoretical analysis. This might seem attractive to analysts, but for psychologists and computer scientists who desire to test or apply the theory, their theory lacked a formalization of this essential last step.

Another point of critique is the fact that all analyses are based on information that is present in the musical score, whereas it is far from certain if, and to what extent, a score is a perceptual reality, that is, a reflection of what the listener experiences. (I will return to this later.)

SPECIFYING KNOWLEDGE: FORMALIZATION

Despite this, Lerdahl and Jackendoff's theory had a major impact. Their book is the most cited music theoretical publication of the last fifty years. But it is not the music theorists and musicologists—with whom it met a mixed reception—who cite it most. It is the computer scientists and psychologists, who welcomed it as offering the beginning of a formal description of musicological analyses and clear points of departure for verifiable hypotheses. The result of all of this is that Lerdahl and Jackendoff's theory has been widely debated and further formalized and tested.

Less well known is the fact that their theory in turn has influenced linguistics. During the 1990s, linguists Alan Prince and Paul

Smolensky, who were seeking language models based more on perception and cognition, found inspiration in Lerdahl and Jackendoff's theory for the development of their own *Optimality Theory*, an alternative for Chomskyan grammars. In it, they described the interpretation of linguistic utterances as the result of competition between different possibilities. And so, once again, the deficiency in musicology's "balance sheet" was adjusted, a deficiency caused because insights and methods that were more often borrowed from other disciplines, were now given back to them.

All in all, Lerdahl and Jackendoff's theory is a worthy example of the role that *formalization*—the specifying and making explicit of knowledge—can play in communicating knowledge. By formalizing knowledge and insights, they also become available for interpretation outside the original discipline. It may not be particularly urgent for musicologists to formalize basic notions such as "meter" or "tempo"; these are, after all, "merely" points of departure (or *axioms*) on which many, inherently much more interesting, musical issues are based. But this is not the case for researchers in related fields, like music perception or cognition; for them, these fundamental, music-theoretical concepts and anything a specific theory has to say about them are of central importance.

Formalization opens up knowledge by making it specific, thereby minimalizing the scope for our individual interpretations. The latter is particularly important because knowledge is often concealed in our interpretations, knowledge that remains invisible to those who don't have access to it; after all, you don't know what has been interpreted or how you did it. For this reason, the interpretation must also be specified and made explicit. Others are then able to verify the conclusions or formulate alternatives that may lead to the same results.

This is one of the primary reasons so much emphasis is placed on formalization in the sciences. During formalization, it is possible to establish whether a concept has been properly thought out or not: if it hasn't, an explicit and verifiable definition will simply be absent.

Imagine, as a music psychologist, that you are interested in musical tempi. Which concrete aspects make one part of the music sound fast and another part slow? Is it the number of notes per minute? Is it a case of "the more notes per second, the faster the music?" A listening experiment quickly shows it is not as simple as that.

A computational musicologist would tackle the mystery of tempo differently. In the first place, he would ask himself what the algorithm should be based on that would sort all the music files on his computer. He would, for instance, quickly realize that it is not always the regularity with which the volume meter sweeps to the right that determines the tempo. That would be appropriate for techno, but not for reggae. So what *does* determine it then?

For musicians, or musicologists, the tempo of music is anything but a mystery; they hear the tempo of a piece, the *tactus*, immediately, and grasp the tempo the conductor will keep. But that knowledge, shared by all music experts, remains elusive in the literature. Today's music encyclopedias still limit themselves to cultural-historical descriptions of (the development of) the concept of "tempo." Tempo as perceived by the listener is not discussed; it is taken for granted, as if it were unworthy of scientific scrutiny.

Even in Lerdahl and Jackendoff's theory, a definition of tempo remains implicit. Although the authors clearly demonstrate a relationship between the concepts of "*tactus*" and "metrical structure," they restrict themselves to music as it appears in the score. Tempo plays a nominal role in their theory, as do "timing" and "intonation," to mention only two other aspects that are not notated in the score. Lerdahl and Jackendoff's music theory, and the theories related to it, abstract away from the perceived music, just as linguistics, which analyses *written* texts, and abstracts away from the spoken word and, as such, reduces speech to a set of symbols.

Even today, symbols ordered in tree structures remain central to both the Chomskyan research program and the relatively young statistical or probabilistic approaches to language and music. But they are often presented in opposite ways. Whereas Chomskyan theory assumes an inborn generative grammar, data-oriented theories emphasize the role of implicit (or explicit) learning. Both, however, assume that their objects—language and music respectively—can be reduced to a set of letters, i.e., symbols. In the same way as a text comprises letters, so a score comprises notes.

This assumption has, of course, the great advantage that the syntax of language *and* music can be described and understood in analogous ways. Lerdahl and Jackendoff's work represents a good example of this.

The question remains, however, whether this supposition is generally applicable. While in practice we see it is possible to represent music and language in letters and symbols, respectively, in music cognition it is doubtful whether these symbols (read: notes) are basic units of meaning that can be ordered in a tree structure. It may well be that the trees of modern linguistics obfuscates the forest of music.

DOES MUSIC HAVE AN ALPHABET?

The title of this section is "Ooh-ooh-ooh." One assumes it reads easily. But read it again, as if it were meant to be sung. How would you pronounce it then? How would it sound, and what would it mean? Probably like a group of letters with no clear meaning—that is, if you've never heard it before and it evokes no associations.

The meaning of "Ooh-ooh-ooh," like that of "Wow!" "Aw," and "Hmm," lies in the nuances of the shifts in tone, sound, and rhythm with which it is uttered; it is they that give meaning to these otherwise meaningless sounds. As long as "Ooh-ooh-ooh" remains a group of individual letters that cannot be "sung" free of the paper on which they're written, it is anyone's guess what they mean. In short, letters alone are not enough to capture the musical aspects of such a sound.

In linguistics, it is an accepted idea that the essence of spoken language can be captured in a series of independent letters or symbols. Linguistics substantiates this by studying the relationship between the visual manifestations of language and its meaning, and by unleashing innumerable logical and mathematical operations onto texts. The result was the Chomskyan revolution mentioned earlier.

In other areas of linguistics, particularly phonology, there is an awareness of the limitations of reducing language to a series of independent symbols. But, for the time being, it isn't seen as a fundamental problem, the more so because numerous studies have proven that there is a lot to be learned about grammar, meaning and language usage from a symbolic approach. So how does it work with music?

Both classical music theory and modern musicology (the latter inspired by language theory) study music as a series of symbols: as notes with a pitch and a duration that can be precisely described:

for example, "a crochet C followed by a quaver G" (that is, the first two notes of Figure 4.1, see p. 31). In music, too, "text"—the musical notation—plays a key role.

Western musical notation is an excellent example of an attempt to formalize music and to record on paper in a precise and unequivocal fashion what the composer wants us to hear. Nevertheless, this script continues to be more of a performance protocol than a representation of music. It contains exact—and sometimes less exact—instructions for how a piece of music is to be performed, but not for what is to be performed. Moreover, it is designed to be read easily from the sheet.

A rhythm, for example, is often encoded in two different ways at the same time. Absolutely, with flags on stems, indicating the relative duration (the more flags, the shorter the note). And proportionally, with longer notes more widely spaced on the paper than shorter notes. All this is to ensure that as our eyes move from left to right, we can easily read the score. For a computer, one code would suffice.

At the same time, many musicologists continue to cherish music notation as a valuable treasure. And there's good reason for this. With great effort they have learned to read clefs, flats, sharps, flags, and so on, and to convert them in their minds into notes, harmonies, and timbres. Paper becomes music; a magical trick that many a layman or enthusiast would give his eye-tooth for!

Some musicologists and composers even go so far as to view the compositional relationships between the notes encoded in the music notation as more important than the actual listening and listening experience. Their analyses and aesthetic descriptions are based on "the relationships between the sounds as represented by the composer and interpreted by the musician, analyst and listener." This is comparable to the cook who tastes the meal on his tongue just by reading the recipe. So why is it, then, that reading musical scores has never become as popular as reading books?

Letters and words form the basis of many interpretations and analyses. Drawing on our vocabulary and knowledge of grammar, we read books without feeling we're missing something. We imagine anything, we tease words into images, the stories take place in our heads.

But, compared to language, all of this is much less applicable to music notation. In recent decades, music lovers have enthusiastically embraced a great variety of new sound carriers, while musical scores have been ignored. Score reading and *audiation* (as in imagination) has limited itself to a small group of professional musicians, who resort to a score when they are unable to make the music them-selves or when they want to hear a particular piece performed with different instruments.

For most people, there is a huge difference between "paper music" and the actual listening experience. A score reader cannot fully (or usually) evoke or construct this experience by reading a score, as he does when reading a book. In this sense, musical scores fail; they are unsuitable for facilitating the musical experience and therefore also as a basis for any research aiming to come to grips with listening and the listening experience.

WHAT A LITTLE MOONLIGHT CAN DO

"Ooh-ooh-ooh"—we "heard" this earlier in the chapter. These are the opening sounds of a recording by Billie Holiday, the jazz singer who was all the rage in the 1950s. They were followed by the beguilingly rhyming *"What a little moonlight can do"*: words and sounds that can instantly brighten your spirits (several versions of this song can be found on the Internet, the live version from 1958 being my favourite).

If you look at the transcription of this opening text, you will see little more than three "ooh's." In combination with "moonlight," these apparently meaningless sounds acquire a kind of meaning after all. But it is virtually impossible to reduce them meaningfully to individual notes. Where does one note begin and the other end? It is fruitless to attempt it; the meaning of "ooh-ooh-ooh" is better sought in the (indivisible) whole than in the individual sounds and notes.

This example demonstrates how letters, and language in general, fall short here. Ray Jackendoff and a number of others dismiss melodic utterances like "oh," "wow," and "hey" as relics from the "one-word stage" of language. Still others emphasize, in my view rightfully, that such expressions represent a fundamental and very old aspect of language—which may even be a sign that music predates language.

"Ooh-ooh-ooh" is a good example of what linguist Alison Wray and archaeologist Steven Mithen refer to when they talk of a "protolanguage": a kind of "sung language" that preceded our present-day music and modern language (an idea going back to Darwin, Rousseau, and others). Unlike what Jackendoff suggests, they aren't loose words searching for a grammar but, rather, indivisible expressions of human emotion. Such melodic forms of expression may well touch on the essence of music, which would reduce the previously mentioned tree structures to "syntactic sugar," which is yet another reason to prefer Pinker's "sweet cheesecake" to Chomsky's syntactic sugar!

EVOLUTION OF LANGUAGE AND MUSIC

Parallels between language and music are also touched on in the discussion about their place in evolution. Whereas Pinker sees music as a side-effect of language, others assume music and language to share a common origin, having evolved from a prehistoric protolanguage. The inverse of Pinker's idea is also conceivable: language as a side-effect of music (*protomusic as the precursor to cultivated music and language*, as suggested in Chapter 1). And, lastly, there's the variation: music and language have no relationship with each other at all, each having their own origin.

The drawback of all these alternatives is that they are doomed to remain theories. Music doesn't fossilize. Neither do our musical brains. Because of this, more recent research programs are advocating concentrating on the *here and now*, and particularly on the language- and music-related skills of humans and other animals. Comparative biological research may be useful here, because it can

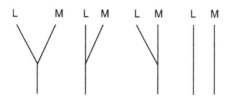

Figure 4.3 Ways in which language (L) and music (M) could have evolved. (Time runs from bottom to top.)

clearly identify the biological functions involved in musicality, and the extent to which humans share these functions with other species. I will consider several possible candidates in the next chapter.

Different views of the relationship between music and language also exist in the neurosciences. There, the primary question is the extent to which music and language can be said to involve identical brain functions, and whether language and music capacities can be situated at the same location in the brain. Some researchers believe different areas of the brain are involved in each function. They base their opinions on case studies of people with brain damage who have lost their ability to speak while their musical skills remained intact, and vice versa; this is known as the modularity hypothesis. In contrast, other researchers emphasize that music and language share both brain functions and locations. Among other things, this opinion is based on the obvious fact that musical and linguistic activities influence each other, particularly in the area of syntax; this is the so-called resource-sharing hypothesis.

The discussion continues today (see Further reading). There's a lot that can be said about it, but one thing is clear: the popular notion that music can be localized in the right half of the brain and language in the left is utter nonsense. When we listen to music, numerous areas throughout the brain are involved.

But before proceeding, allow me to remind you of the four main differences between music and language (summarized in Box 4.1).

In the first place, music has no *syntaxis*. That is to say, it will not allow itself to be divided into grammatical and non-grammatical structures the way language does. A lot, if not everything, is possible in music. Although there is such a thing as "well-formed" music, the nature of its rules, even for tonal music, is much less restrictive than the rules for language. Ultimately, it is the listener who "hears music" in something. Compositional rules determine which genre a piece of music belongs to, but *not* whether the piece has meaning or not.

Secondly, music has no *semantics*; that is, it lacks semantics as it is intertwined with syntax in language. Labels attributing meaning A or B to a melody are not usually applied in music. The meaning of music resides mostly in the pitch movement, rhythm, and timing. The individual notes themselves are meaningless. *C'est le ton qui fait la musique.*

Thirdly, music seems to appeal much more directly to the emotions than language. "Sung music" in particular, with all its tonal modulations and variations in timing, is (almost) experienced as a holistic whole. The development of the melody and the way the rhythm is articulated are the "carriers" of that emotional "meaning."

Lastly, music cannot be captured in an alphabet the way language, miraculously enough, can. In the best-case scenario, a composition as recorded in a score is like a cookbook: it includes instructions on the "what" and "how," but it has no influence on the tasting, savouring, and enjoying of the resulting (musical) meals. In this sense, music cannot be put into words. How problematic is that?

THE INEFFABILITY OF MUSIC

Philosophers like Arthur Schopenhauer and Suzanne Langer and, more recently, Diana Raffman were convinced: music can only partially be put into words. According to Raffman, the ineffability of music, especially of the listening experience, comprises at least two elements: that which cannot be remembered and that which cannot be said.

Some nuances in music, like a singer's specific timing or intonation, resist allowing themselves to be stored in memory. You may remember experiencing them in a certain way (the emotion is traceable), but the whole musical experience, the performance in all its details, doesn't last. Nuances in the performance can be heard and experienced but—again according to Raffman—not precisely recalled, distinguished, or named. We simply don't have the categories and concepts that allow us to put these sensorial experiences into words. A performance can be heard, experienced, and appreciated, but it is impossible after the event to recount exactly what was experienced during the performance. Music critics will vouch for this.

There is a great temptation to make an absolute of the so-called "ineffability" of music. Many have succumbed to it. Ineffable, however, is not the same as ungraspable, which would ultimately mean that music cannot be studied scientifically. This, too, is a classical misunderstanding. Though it may be difficult to describe the taste of a tomato, particularly the unique taste of a biologically cultivated vine tomato, most people can still taste the difference.

In short, "putting into words" is not a prerequisite for understanding listening. To which one might add: it is difficult, in practice, to capture in words or symbols especially those aspects that are essential to the appreciation of a musical performance. They are, in fact, inexpressible, whereby any comparison between music and language becomes useless from the scientific-philosophical and methodological perspective. It is therefore wise to leave the description of music for what it is and to look at music as a sonologist would do: as a unique kind of sound.

BOX 4.1   DIFFERENCES BETWEEN MUSIC AND LANGUAGE

1   Music does not allow itself to be divided into grammatical and non-grammatical structures the way language does. Although there is such a thing as "well-formed" music, the nature of its rules, even for tonal music, is much less restrictive than the rules for language. There is no such thing as "a wrong melody."

2   Music has no *semantics*, in the sense that it is intertwined with *syntaxis* or word order (like in English "Man bites dog" means something different than "Dog bites man"). The meaning of music resides mostly in the intonation, dynamics, and timing (*musical prosody*).

3   While language addresses the ratio at first, music often appeals directly to emotions.

4   Music cannot be fully captured in an alphabet and words. At best, a musical score is like a cookbook; an instruction of "what" and "how" with little or no influence on how it is experienced.

SUMMARY

Like in language, structure plays a role in music. But while most languages are made up of an alphabet (letters), words (*idiom*), and grammar (*syntaxis*), music appears to lack an alphabet. Important musical aspects, like intonation, tempo, and timing, stay implicit. This observation also holds for Lerdahl and Jackendoff's well-known theory of tonal music, in which music is restricted to its appearance in the score. Nevertheless, their classic theory shows how formalization can make musical knowledge explicit, and as such make it available for interdisciplinary interpretation.

FURTHER READING

Bernstein, L. (1976). *The Unanswered Question*. Cambridge, MA: The MIT Press.

Lerdahl, F. & Jackendoff, R. (1983). *A Generative Theory of Tonal Music*. Cambridge, MA: The MIT Press.

Patel, A. D. (2010). *Music, Language and the Brain*. Oxford: Oxford University Press.

MUSIC AS SOUND

What are the differences between music and sound? Why could this be interesting for music scientists?

Sound is an important aspect of music. It is significant that the music industry has had almost a century of success in selling encoded sound vibrations on carriers such as records, cassettes, and CDs or in the form of MP3 files. No one complains that something is missing in these solidified vibrations, although avid concertgoers might point to the absence of the concert hall (the physical), of the shared listening experience (the collective), and of the chats during the interval (the social). But, musically speaking, the music registered in all its detail on the sound carriers seems to be complete.

"Music as sound" would appear to be an appropriate general characterization, particularly against the background of recent Western music history. The idea dates from the time when accepted definitions of music badly needed to be expanded. In the 1950s, composers like Edgar Varèse, Karlheinz Stockhausen, and John Cage in particular explored the limits of what, until then, the average listener had called "music."

The result was mostly music in which the percussion dominated (unparalleled in classical music), or in which not a single "real" instrument could be heard because it was produced totally electronically (using the earliest recording equipment and synthesizers). Music produced largely by chance also formed part of the modern repertoire. The result of all this was that the definition of music came under heavy pressure. Even Varèse's proposal to describe it as "organized sound" proved untenable and had to be reconsidered as early as 1952.

DOI: 10.4324/9781003158301-7

MUSIC IS NOT SOUND

The differences between music and sound, like those between music and language, can also help us clarify what it is that makes music so special. There is every reason not to equate music with sound. Whoever defines music as vibrations in the air with a specific structure that we then interpret as music only adds to the confusion. Such a definition assumes that sound is either the source—the factual object—or the carrier of music. But there are plenty of arguments against this.

In the first place, we recognize the same piece of music whether played to us via a hi-fi installation or reaching us via a crackly regular telephone connection from the other side of the ocean. The quality of the sound may be poorer, but the music remains the same: in both cases, we hear the same melody, the same harmony, and the same rhythmic structure. Which is why high-tech sound-installation enthusiasts listen to *more* than just the music: they listen to their installation too.

In other words, sound and sound quality are not the determining factors in what makes music music. The acoustic laws of sound tell us nothing about music, with the exception of music whose primary substance is timbre, as is the case with some recent electronic music.

Secondly, sound is not a carrier of music. The concept of "music" always implies a potential listener, and if you define music solely in terms of sound, there is no listener.

The definition of music as "organized sound"—plied primarily by many composers and musicologists—raises a similar objection. The methods that have taken root in that discipline are largely *data-oriented*, based on the idea (or hope) that all relevant information is contained in the (measured) sound signals, the "data." Unfortunately, it isn't as simple as that.

Let me give an example: searching for music files on the Internet is just as complicated as searching for images. To "read" images, you use a lot more information than you actually see: for example, a lot of information is not contained in the image itself but is created through our perception and cognition. Think of perspective in painting or depth of field in photography: we automatically make a distinction between a wineglass in the foreground and a wineglass in the background. It remains a major challenge for contemporary computer software to get a grip on this kind of supplementary information.

It is no different with music. It is a misconception to think, as some computer scientists do, that all relevant musical information is encoded in the sound signal (and on a sound carrier like the CD). The listener adds all kinds of crucial information not contained in the data, by using their cognitive predispositions and listening experience to make sense of the sound signal. For instance, to be able to appreciate a syncopation, an exciting groove, a catchy melody, or unexpected note. These are exactly the things we are interested in, at least in this book.

A third objection to the definition of music as "sound" is that music can also involve silence. A well-known example is John Cage's 1952 composition *4'33"*, which has come to be regarded as iconoclastic evidence for the expanded definition of music. Aside from its important role in recent music history, to this day Cage's composition attests to the notion that the listener plays an important role in what makes music music.

For those not familiar with the composition: a pianist arrives on stage, closes the keyboard lid of the piano and proceeds to do nothing at all for the next four minutes and thirty-three seconds, then opens the lid again and leaves the stage. The listener, in fact, does all the work.

With this beautifully chosen dramatic form, Cage clearly illustrates that music resides primarily, to use his words, "in the intention of listening." Concertgoers listen to all the chance sounds, from the rhythm of the breathing public to the noise of a passing tram or ambulance, *as if* they were music. The listener makes the music, whether or not there is sound.

And lastly, the definition of music as "sound" wrongly suggests that music, like all natural phenomena, adheres to the laws of nature. In this case, the laws would be the acoustical patterns of sound such as the (harmonic) relationships in the structure of the dominant tones, which determine the timbre. This is an idea that has preoccupied primarily the mathematically oriented music scientists, from Pythagoras to Hermann von Helmholtz. The first, and oldest, of these scientists, Pythagoras (570–495 BC), observed, for example, that "beautiful" consonant intervals consist of simple frequency relationships (such as 2:3 or 3:4). Several centuries later, Galileo Galilei (1564–1642) wrote that complex frequency relationships only "tormented" the eardrum.

But, for all their wisdom, Pythagoras, Galilei, and like-minded thinkers got it wrong. In music, the "beautiful," so-called "whole-number" frequency relationships rarely occur—in fact, only when a composer dictates them. The composer often even must have special instruments built to achieve them, as American composer Harry Partch (1901–1974) did in the twentieth century.

Contemporary pianos are tuned in such a way that the sounds produced only approximate all those beautiful "natural" relationships. The tones of the instrument do not have simple whole number ratios, as in 2:3 or 3:4. Instead, they are tuned so that every octave is divided into twelve equal parts (so-called *12 equal temperament*, a compromise to facilitate changes of key). The tones exist, therefore, not as whole number ratios of each other, but as multiples of $12\sqrt{2}$ (≈ 1.05946).

According to Galilei, each and every one of these frequency relationships are "a torment" to the ear. But modern listeners experience them very differently. It seems that our ears have easily adapted to the "dissonant" frequencies of our Western *equal temperament* tuning system. One might even conclude that the tuning of a piano is irrelevant to our appreciation of music.

Of course, this does not mean we are insensitive to the tuning and intonation of music. On the contrary, we instantly hear small modulations in pitch. But the tuning of an instrument—such as the exact frequency number of each note of the piano—is clearly less important. This tuning produces a framework within which a specific intonation becomes meaningful, but the framework itself, the tuning of the instrument as a whole, gets less of the listener's attention.

Compare it to a poor-quality color television set or an old black-and-white film. With the television, you quickly adjust to the strange colors: you know that the playing field is made of grass, despite its red glow. With a black-and-white film, familiarity with something else makes you aware of the absence of color, but this only lasts for a few moments, and you quickly begin to distinguish fine shades of grey. When experiencing an image, elements other than "color" are clearly more important.

The same applies to music and the specific tuning methods used: we adapt quickly to the tuning, just as we adapt quickly to the "strange" colors of an old color television set, but we retain our sensitivity to the intonation and timing. I will return to this repeatedly: it is the *relative* aspects of music to which our perception and cognition are receptive, not the literal, *absolute* aspects such as sound, frequency, and pitch.

MUSIC AS NUMBERS

There is something nostalgic and romantic about approaching music as a natural and mathematical phenomenon: it echoes the ancient Greek notion of the "harmony of the spheres," as if we might return to that time (in so far as it ever existed), when harmonic, beautiful, or "true" music was determined by nature. All we must do is decipher the harmonic number ratios concealed in music, and then, just like Pythagoras, we too will be able to link music with the cosmos!

The idea that the mathematical structure of music can reveal something about nature itself continues to appear, though in different guises, together with the notion that a sophisticated formula that breaks the code of Bach or Mozart's music and exposes its underlying numerical structure can show us how beautiful and "natural" that music is: the golden ratio, numerology, *The Mystery of* ... countless books have been written about it. But it is all wisdom after the fact. They are not explanations, but interpretations, objectifications gone too far, overshooting the mark.

It may be strange to hear this from a practitioner of the exact sciences. Let me qualify it with an important nuance: the pursuit of order in nature and in the nature of things says little about the music we hear, but it says a lot about the abstractions we love to project on to music. We ourselves play an active and leading role in what we hear and perceive, in which we make use of our memory, our observations, and our expectations. In this sense, every listening experience is subjective. It is not, however, an experience based on chance (our impressions of music overlap too frequently for that), and it is an experience that can be scientifically studied. Sound patterns are, at most, a starting point, never an endpoint.

For a long time, I, too, was convinced that scientists like Huygens and Helmholtz and composers like Stockhausen and Varèse were on the right track when they took the mathematical structure of music as a starting point. But several things severely undermined my faith in this: my first experiences in making music with computers (during a study of sonology), polymath Christopher Longuet-Higgins's pioneering work on the computational modelling of music cognition (see Chapter 9), and my own first attempts to construct a "listening" and "conducting" computer (more on this in Chapter 14).

I now no longer believe that music can be studied separately from the listener. If there is no listener, there is no music. This is not to say, however, that mathematics is no longer relevant; it continues to be an important tool in enhancing our understanding of music and listening.

In summary, music is not sound, it is *listening* to sound. Both the music "heard" and the musical "hearer" are needed if we are to understand what makes music music. This is why, in the following chapters, I will not work with the notions of "music as language" or "music as sound," but will approach music as "cognition" and assign the listener a key role!

So let us leave the stage now and take our seat in the concert hall.

BOX 5.1. FOUR REASONS WHY MUSIC IS NOT THE SAME AS SOUND

1 Whether we hear music via a supersonic hi-fi system or through a crackly phone connection, we recognize the melody, harmony, and rhythmic structure of a piece of music.

2 Music doesn't obey the natural laws of sound, like many acoustical phenomena do. Pythagoras' admired whole-numbered frequency relationships rarely occur in music.

3 Music also involves the opposite of sound—silence.

4 When defining music as (organized) sound, one ignores the fundamental role of the listener.

SUMMARY

Like the differences between music and language, the differences between music and sound also help us to define music. In the twentieth century the electrification of sound started a revolution in music; on the one hand by composers who invented electronical compositions, and on the other hand by the industry producing novel music carriers and hi-fi systems. Still, to believe that all relevant musical information can be encoded in sound signals is a misconception. Music involves much more than sound. In fact, the listener, with their predispositions and listening experience, turns sound into music.

FURTHER READING

Von Helmholtz, H. (1863; 1954). *On the Sensations of Tone as a Physiological Basis for the Theory of Music*. New York: Dover Publications.
Sethares, W. A. (2005). *Tuning, Timbre, Spectrum, Scale*. Berlin: Springer.

PART 3

HMMM ... :
MUSIC AND MUSICALITY

WE'RE MUSICAL CREATURES

What is musicality? What skills do we need to appreciate music? Do other animals have these as well? What makes a great musician?

There are many misunderstandings about musicality. People who consider themselves to be unmusical, say that they have no feel for rhythm or that they can't sing in tune. And they are quick to view birdsong, or a cockatoo that can dance in time to music, as "musical." But can animals really be musical? What is musicality, actually?

In one of the documentaries that Dutch filmmaker Bert Haanstra filmed in a Dutch zoo some twenty years ago, there is a sequence in which a group of lowland gorillas are playing music together, or rather, that's what the editing suggests. First, we see a shot of a gorilla drumming enthusiastically on a large barrel. Clearly, as he is looking around much as an orchestral conductor would do, he is the leader of the band. Then another gorilla comes into view, rhythmically beating its chest, followed by a third gorilla that is repeatedly gliding its fingers up and down over its lips to make a rhythmical plopping noise. It's obvious that all three animals are thoroughly enjoying themselves.

In their natural habitat there are many kinds of apes that spontaneously drum on tree trunks and on other objects. There is even a recorded incident of a male ape making so much noise on an oil drum, that he was able to climb up the social hierarchy of his group to become its leader. In this case, "music" was used as a means to impress or gain power. But is it really music? Are these apes really musical? The answer is "yes and no."

DOI: 10.4324/9781003158301-9

No matter how much we would like it to be different, we are repeatedly reminded that we have more similarities to animals than differences. However, we must be careful in calling a chimpanzee's drumming on an empty barrel, music. We make this mistake too often. We, the human listeners, perceive the sounds made by creatures such as songbirds, whales, or chimpanzees as music. Whether these creatures also do that, or whether they experience the same amount of pleasure in the sounds they themselves produce is questionable. And that makes a world of difference! The essence of music and musicality lies not so much in producing it as in listening to it.

There have been many enthusiastic attempts in the past to demonstrate that animals have musical talent, and people have also tried to teach apes the rudiments of language. Some time ago, a study appeared about the Asiatic elephants that were brought together to form the *Thai Elephant Orchestra*. These images appeal to the imagination: the elephant that was filmed could rhythmically, or rather, regularly strike a drum with a stick by holding it in its trunk. Unfortunately, though, the speed with which it did that was probably more closely related to the "natural frequency" of its own trunk—the preferred speed with which the elephant swings its trunk back and forth—than with the tempo maintained by the rest of the elephants in the orchestra. What the elephants didn't do was to actually listen.

Although the Asiatic elephants do something that, to our ears, resembles music, they are nevertheless totally unreceptive to the frequency of the drums of their fellow musicians. If you were to try and get them to play a little bit slower, you would find that they couldn't.

These, and all other elephants, lack one of the most fundamental elements that makes music accessible to human beings: the ability to hear the beat. In almost all human beings, this sensitivity for the regularity of a rhythm is inborn. However, so far, it has proved impossible to get other creatures, including our closest relatives in the animal kingdom—chimpanzees and lowland gorillas—to drum, clap, or dance along with us (see Chapter 7).

THERE IS NO MUSIC WITHOUT MUSICALITY

Of course, before we can assess whether an animal species is able to both make and experience music, we first need a definition of what music actually is. But then, there are quite a number of possible definitions. These range from considering music as "organized sound" to anything that "sounds like music."

One thing is certain: music includes everything that we consider to be music, or rather, everything in which we hear music. *Music is in the mind of the listener.* We readily experience birdsong as music, but this does not mean that it is also music for the birds *themselves.* The same applies to humpback whales, dolphins, and other animals that make sounds which we like to interpret as music.

To avoid misunderstandings and different interpretations, it is useful, therefore, to make a strict distinction between "musicality" and "music." By "musicality" we understand as a natural, spontaneously developing set of traits that are based on and constrained by our cognitive abilities and its underlying biology. We define "music," on the other hand, as a social and cultural construct based on that very musicality. Hence, without musicality, there can be no music. With this important distinction, it is possible to talk about musicality without broaching the question of what is, or is not meant by "music."

For someone to enjoy music, what are the listening skills needed? What kind of knowledge or skills do you need to perceive, appreciate, and remember music?

Although musicality is viewed by many as an exceptional talent, in fact, the fundamental building blocks of musicality can be found in every person. Musicality is largely based on qualities present in everyone from birth, such as the ability to recognize and appreciate melodies and rhythms. The fundamental elements in this are the ability to hear regularity and to recognize melodies. In this book, I shall call them by their technical terms, respectively, *beat induction* and *relative pitch.* Both are prerequisites for experiencing music as music rather than sound.

In addition, to differentiate and appreciate music, sensitivity to all kinds of musical nuances is necessary. A classical piano sonata can be played in all manner of ways, even though, at every performance, the notes are exactly the same, and are played in exactly the same order. A pop singer can also give a song a completely different emphasis, by applying his or her unique timing and intonation. A few small variations in the tempo, and we can tell immediately that the pianist has had a classical training. A tiny jerk in the voice and we can hear immediately that there is a country and western singer behind the microphone.

This sensitivity to musical nuances is an essential element of musicality. These are all listening skills common to almost everyone, and that function as the building blocks of music. Although there are, of course, exceptions that prove the rule: people who claim to be unmusical.

BEING UNMUSICAL

What makes someone unmusical? Quite a lot of research has been carried out into this topic recently. There is even a special test to determine if someone is unmusical. The condition is known as *amusia*, and those who suffer from it are literally music deficient. It is a rather exceptional, mostly inherited condition that comprises a range of handicaps in recognizing melodies and rhythms. It has been estimated that about one to two percent of the people in Western Europe and North America have amusia, to a greater or lesser degree. The most common handicap is *tone-deafness*: the inability or difficulty in hearing the difference between two separate melodies.

To diagnose amusia, the Montreal Battery of Evaluation of Amusia (MBEA) has been developed. This test is available on the Internet—but wait a while before searching for it. It appears that people often diagnose themselves mistakenly as suffering from amusia. In fact, about 15 percent of the population think they have this condition, although the percentage of truly tone-deaf people is no higher than one or two percent. So, it actually affects only a very small section of the population. People who say: "I can't hold a note," "I sing out of tune," or "I have no sense of rhythm," are not necessarily suffering from amusia. Such people often confuse poor singing skills with the absence of a sense of hearing differences in melodies.

If someone sings out of tune, this is usually due to lack of practice, rather than to the absence of a cognitive skill for handling musical material. If you ask a random selection of people in the street to sing a song, and compare that with professional singers who sing the same song, then, indeed, the first group will appear to make more mistakes than the second one. The mistakes will be mainly in the melody: a note sung a little bit too high or too low compared with the original. Song *rhythms*, on the other hand, are usually reproduced just as well by amateurs as by professionals.

If you ask the same sample of singers to sing the song in a quiet place and at a somewhat slower tempo, then the differences disappear. The mistakes appear to be caused more by haste than by poor singing skills. In general, therefore, people have better inborn singing skills than was first thought.

The study referred to above investigates musicality while music is being performed. In this book, however, I concentrate mainly on musicality while listening. In the discussion about musicality, these two aspects are often confused. Production, the making of music, is tricky and demands a lot of practice. In Chapter 1, I called it the "acrobatics" of music making. And not everyone is cut out for such acrobatics.

Perception, listening to music, is another story altogether. It seems that only very few people are unmusical in that respect, and the differences between musical experts and lay people are much smaller than generally thought. Even though the expert may be better able to name and label specific musical aspects, as far as the actual listening skills are concerned, neither group outperforms the other.

More importantly: it is not so much the musical expertise, but the mere contact with music, being exposed to it, that appears to be the important factor. Sometimes, lay people listen better than experts do, simply because they are more familiar with a certain genre they like to listen to a lot.

Also, rhythmic behaviour—like clapping, drumming, dancing—is often confused with listening. Clapping a complex rhythm requires quite some practice; nevertheless, almost all of us can *hear* the differences between rhythms. It has been established that, even in people who are known to have amusia, most of them have a normal sense for rhythm.

Finally, it appears that people with amusia are often sensitive to the emotional message in a melody. Even though they might not be able to hear whether a certain note in a melody is sung higher or lower, they can sense whether the tune is sad or happy. Amusia is associated more with tone-deafness than with deafness to every aspect of music.

In recent research, the British neuropsychologist Lauren Stewart investigated whether people with amusia can listen to music with pleasure. The responses to questionnaires were not always positive: "Music can irritate me a lot. I ask myself then what other people feel, and wonder whether I'm missing something." Or: "Sometimes the words of songs from my youth make me nostalgic. But I can't listen to them; I have to read the words instead."

The intriguing outcome of this research suggests that consciously perceiving and appreciating music are two separate activities that have little to do with each other. In some situations it appears that there are large differences between people with and without amusia: for instance, people with amusia are usually irritated by music at parties. But in many other social situations, these same amusia sufferers experience and appreciate music in much the same way as "normal" listeners. This applies particularly to film music, which is often played to create or strengthen the sphere or mood of the occasion. The emotional message of the music is thus reasonably well appreciated by a large proportion of the people with amusia. So even though there are deficiencies in their overall perception, enough remains to make listening worthwhile.

Music lovers will probably find it difficult to imagine, but there are also people for whom music means nothing at all: people who never deliberately listen to music, and if they hear it, are unmoved. It is referred to as *musical anhedonia,* a neurological condition characterized by an inability to derive pleasure from music. Only recently researchers have been investigating this intriguing group of listeners. Personally, I have only met two: a librarian and a journalist. The latter claimed never to enjoy playing music while at home, and if she listened to the radio, then it was mainly to a news channel. She said she wasn't annoyed by music, but it was more that she simply didn't get anything out of it. However, she admitted to being jealous from time to time of people for whom music means a great deal.

MUSICAL TALENT

The opposite of amusia is an overdeveloped sensitivity to perceiving, remembering, and performing music. Examples that come immediately to mind are people with autism or Williams syndrome, who show an exceptional, often spontaneously developed talent for music. There are also people who, due to a brain injury suddenly appear to be very musical, or who, from one day to the next, lose their musical skills. These are all exceptional cases that make us realize that our brains have a special link with music.

But how is it with most people? Can one encounter all gradations of musicality in them? Or has the exceptionally talented musician, whether an instrumentalist or a singer, something special that sets them fundamentally apart from all other listeners?

In discussions about musical talent, many examples of child prodigies come to mind. Musical celebrities such as Wolfgang Amadeus Mozart, Stevie Wonder, Beyoncé, Lang Lang, and Tony Williams were already extremely adept musicians at a very young age. It is natural, then, to think that exceptional musical talent is inborn. If that wasn't so, how could the child prodigies named above have developed their musical skills so quickly and at such a young age?

Actually, there is some evidence for the view that exceptional musical talent is determined by our biology. Although genes appear to have an influence on our musical skills; overall, it is mainly (a lot of) practice, perseverance, and an insuppressible urge to play music that are responsible for launching someone into a successful career as a musician. The idea that musical artistry, in the general population, can be attributed solely to an exceptional gene structure is a myth.

Children whose parents have little to do with music can nonetheless develop great musicality, and *vice versa*, it is also evident that having parents who are talented musically is no guarantee that their children will take after them. The majority of world-famous musicians were not child prodigies; they reached the top by playing a great deal of music and by studying in a disciplined way at hours when others are in bed. Although "true" child prodigies seem to develop their talent for music spontaneously, for most musicians, it is more a question of perseverance fed by deep passion.

Gradations in musicality have been proved, for the most part, to be due to a wide range of external factors. For instance, music has a very strong social influence in all cultures. Outside Western Europe, though, its influence has often been even wider. If you ask someone to sing a song at a party in the Netherlands, the only thing that might happen is that the person will blush with embarrassment. In contrast, at a party in Brazil, a guitar will be handed around for everyone to use and they will all have a complete repertoire of *música popular brasileira* ready to perform.

So, although we may have an inborn talent for music, what we do with it is largely determined by our surroundings. The anthropologist John Blacking (1928–1990) considered the elite status given to music by western culture to be a great limitation, while in other cultures, it is the most normal thing in the world to sing, dance, and make music. Perhaps that is why child prodigies and musical experts are noticed so quickly in our culture.

The work of the British music psychologist John Sloboda and his colleagues has greatly clarified the way in which musical talent develops. One of the most important stimulating factors is immersion in music from a very young age. From interviews with talented young musicians, it has become evident that their parents sang to them very frequently and played all sorts of singing games with them when they were children. Although this may not always have had a noticeable effect on how the children played music, it certainly had an effect on their skill in listening to music. For example, children who are brought up with music appear to be better than others at distinguishing between the rhythmic and melodic contrasts in different sorts of music, and that can be extremely helpful during music lessons later on.

In addition, for anyone who aspires to become a professional musician, it is very important to practise a lot. Already, at twenty-one years of age, the average student at a music academy will have practised for more than ten thousand hours. And children who gain admittance to an academy of music will already have studied roughly twice as many hours on their instrument as children who have not passed the selection process. Studying a lot seems to be a crucial condition for success.

Social and emotional factors also make an important contribution to the development of musicality. The first of these, of course, is the environment in which the child grows up. When parents stimulate their children to be enthusiastic about music, encourage them to form a band, organize house concerts, and take them to concerts, that stimulates the development of their passion for music enormously. Bad experiences with a recorder or piano teacher—remarks, with a sigh, that you have *absolutely no talent*, or disdain because of the *terrible noise that you make*—can nip this development in the bud with all the consequences that follow.

The last, and perhaps most surprising, factor is exposure to deep, emotionally loaded musical experiences. Ask musicians to try to remember what prompted their passion for music, and in nine out of ten cases they will tell you, with a radiant expression, about a concert, or some other musical event, at which some exceptional or poignant musical happening took place: "Then I felt that music was important." That kind of strong experience, which strikes like a bolt of lightning, often marks the beginning of a lifelong passion for music. It is a memory that never goes away; it stays there and feeds musicianship.

Nevertheless, there are reservations about what has just been said. Viewed in totality, it is, of course, not at all surprising that endless practice and conscientious study is an important contribution to exceptional musical talent; the same applies to successes in sport, art, politics, and science. It is the skills that develop spontaneously, without much practice or many formal lessons that are so exceptional. I will focus below on two of these skills, both of which we all possess: beat induction and relative pitch. These are skills that most people take for granted, although, in actual fact, they are really quite exceptional. They form the basis of *music and musicality*.

BOX 6.1   MUSICAL ANIMALS

Charles Darwin, the famous evolutionary biologist, assumed that all animals perceive and appreciate rhythm and melody, simply because they have comparable nervous systems. He was therefore convinced that human musicality had a biological basis. He also suggested that sensitivity to music must be an extremely old trait, much older than sensitivity to language. In fact, he viewed musicality as the source of both music and language, and attributed its presence in humans and animals to the evolutionary mechanism of *sexual selection* (see Chapter 1). However, only recently researchers have found evidence in support of Darwin's intuition. The two most notable examples are Snowball, the dancing cockatoo and Ronan, the head-bobbing sea lion (see Chapter 7).

SUMMARY

Music is in the mind of the beholder. Human listeners perceive some sounds made by songbirds, whales, or chimpanzees as music. Whether the animals themselves have the skills to perceive music is questionable. Among humans, musicality is not an exceptional talent. In fact, most of us were born with the fundamental building blocks of musicality, like beat induction and relative pitch. Less than two percent is born with *amusia*: the inability to perceive the beat or melody in music. Musical prodigies like Stevie Wonder, Lang Lang, Beyoncé, and Tony Williams might have had a little more musical genes than most of us, but they would never have reached the top if they hadn't possessed other necessary talents like an intrinsic capability to focus, practise hours a day, and an insuppressible urge to play music.

FURTHER READING

Levitin, D. J. (2012). What does it mean to be musical? *Neuron*, 73 (4), 633–637.
Peretz, I. (2020). *How Music Sculpts Our Brain*. Paris, France: Odile Jacob.

MEASURING THE BEAT

What do you need to perceive the beat in music? Is it an innate ability or is it learned? How do you figure this out scientifically?

As we all know, you can only sing and dance with each other if everyone keeps to the same tempo. Everyone must ensure that he or she sings or moves synchronically with the music. If one person doesn't do that, then it very quickly becomes either a cacophony, or you tread on your partner's feet.

The beat or "*tactus*"—the pulse of the music to which you can tap your foot—doesn't have to be present in the music itself. It is, as it were, evoked while listening; hence the term "beat induction" (also referred to in the scientific literature as *beat inference* or simply *beat-finding*). Because we hear the beat, we notice whether the music is going faster or slower. We hear the rhythmic pattern and its regularities and then base our expectations on that. If we move our feet to the rhythm of the music, then we usually do so a few milliseconds earlier than the beat itself.

All this indicates that beat induction is based on *expectation*. It is an expectation that makes it possible to act anticipatively and proactively: you first have to raise your foot before you can let it come down precisely on the beat. If you have no beat induction, then it's impossible to be in sync with others, so you will be unable to sing, dance, or play music with them.

Most of us cannot avoid hearing the beat in music. In fact, there is very little music that does not have an underlying pulse or beat—unless it is deliberately avoided. In the 1950s, for example, various composers did their level best to remove every element of regularity from their compositions for aesthetic reasons. To do this, they had to

DOI: 10.4324/9781003158301-10

think of many tricks—that contained, by definition, no structure or regularity—ranging from those based on chance to all sorts of mathematical principles, such as mirroring and permutation. These are tricks for which our cognition has no ready-made strategies available to grasp the order in them.

There are musicians who boast that they can recognize a retrograde of a rhythm as being the same rhythm: it's the same thing as understanding a sentence that is spoken back to front. However, that's a very unusual skill and one that can be learnt only to a limited extent. However, the very fact that so much trouble has to be taken to stop us from hearing a beat in music confirms that the beat is a fundamental quality that is present in all of us. It is part of us.

One would therefore expect there to be a lot of support for the idea that beat induction is inborn. But that is not the case. Until recently, the majority of theories proposed beat induction to be an acquired skill. By repeatedly linking music and movement early in a child's development, babies and toddlers can acquire a sense for the regularities in rhythm. For example, parents can cradle their babies or move them to the beat of the music.

According to this view, a sensitivity to the beat is mainly an acquired phenomenon. The consequence of this hypothesis would then be that babies growing up within a certain culture would only be able to synchronize with its music if they had been cradled to it or encouraged by those in their environment to move in time to it. This seems unlikely to me. And even if a good example of such a culture could be found, it wouldn't prove that those babies had no inborn beat induction. Instead, what it could indicate is that a particular inborn skill that is not put to use, may simply become inevident or disappear altogether.

LISTENING BABIES

Beat induction was also one of the core topics in a European research project known as Emergent Cognition through Active Perception (EMCAP). Within this project, research was carried out into how far our cognition is influenced, or perhaps even shaped, by listening to music. One of the planned experiments was to investigate listening in newly born babies. This gave our research group in Amsterdam a fantastic opportunity to collaborate with a research group from the Hungarian Academy of Sciences in Budapest, led by István Winkler, a pioneer in research on hearing in very young babies.

Winkler has quite some experience in the area of *auditory streaming*. He is trying to find out how newly born babies make sense for themselves out of the chaos of sounds around them. Within this context, a frequently asked question is: How do you know what a newly born baby actually hears? After all, it's rather difficult to deduce this from their facial expressions or movements. For adult listeners one can devise all sorts of tasks to test what is going on in their heads, such as pressing buttons, filling in a questionnaire, or comparing different sound examples. However, in the case of newly born babies, there are few visible activities from which to interpret their mental activity. To study this Winkler's group refined a method that utilizes an *electroencephalogram* (EEG) tracing to register the electrical activity in the brain while the baby listens to sounds.

However, an EEG such as this is dominated by all kinds of neural activity that have little to do with reaction to sound or to the music that is being played. For this reason, we looked at the so-called auditory or *event-related potentials* (ERP). These are small sections of the EEG that record tiny responses identifiable by the fact that they occur at a fixed time after the sound signal (the *event*). These can be added up and averaged with the help of a computer, thereby reducing the contribution from other unrelated brain activity, and effectively making the response signal "cleaner."

Interpreting an ERP is an art in itself. In the enormous, mainly medically oriented literature in this area, a richly varied terminology is used to name and interpret the miniscule peaks and troughs in the brain signal that have been measured. For our goal, the most relevant component of the ERP was the *mismatch negativity* (MMN): a small characteristic dip in the brain signal that occurs if something unexpected happens while listening (even during passive listening). For example, it can be seen in the EEG tracing of someone who was presented with a series of tones, similar in duration and pitch, that were interrupted every so often by a tone with a different pitch. About 150–200 milliseconds after an irregularity such as this a small dip can be registered in the brain signal, the MMN.

Discovered in 1978 by the Finnish researcher Riso Näätänen, this phenomenon is viewed as an automatic or unconscious orientation of the brains reflecting the detection of an irregular sound.

MMN turned out to be a reliable measure that indicates whether a certain characteristic of sound, such as pitch, duration, or intensity is incongruous. So you can also use an MMN to calculate how far a listener's expectations have been violated.

Initially, the research team in Budapest was not entirely convinced by this approach, because if you leave a single note out in a series of similar tones, then you do not automatically get an MMN. So the first challenge was to find a rhythm containing an accentuated loud rest: a pause in the music that everyone would notice.[1] If you do the same thing in places where a note is not anticipated, then the rest will pass entirely unnoticed. In short: if a listener hears a loud rest, then it is clear indication of that person having an active sense of rhythm.

After we had tried out a large number of alternatives, our Amsterdam research group finally arrived at a well-known rock rhythm with a strong beat (see Figure 7.1).

Then we devised a number of variations on this rhythm in which notes were omitted in places where there was no beat. In this way, we arrived at a number of rather boring, regular rhythms with rests in places that—theoretically—should go relatively unnoticed; these are given in Figure 7.2.

For the deviant rhythm, we used a rhythmic variation in which the first beat, the *downbeat*, was missing. That has a much more exciting sound. Although the rest in this rhythm lasts just as long as the rests in the other rhythms, music theory states that the rhythm shown below in Figure 7.3 is far more surprising, as it is a deviation away from a strongly expected beat. And because it fails to meet your expectation, it should, then, be easily noticeable.

Figure 7.1 Rock rhythm, as used in the listening experiment on beat induction.

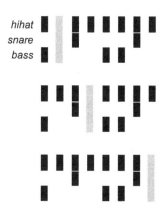

Figure 7.2 Rock rhythms with "quiet rests" (marked with grey bars).

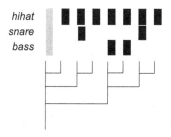

Figure 7.3 A rock rhythm with a "loud rest" (see the grey bar). A metric tree is added underneath the rhythm: the longer the vertical line, the more the emphasis on that particular position in the rhythm.

To test a number of adults' sensitivity to the beat, we asked them to listen to a series of these regular rhythms, and to press a button whenever they heard a deviation in that rhythm: in other words, when they heard a rhythm with a loud rest. That proved to be a simple task, with most of the participants identifying it with ease. And when brain activity was measured while they were presented with this sound sequence, the MMN appeared exactly when the loud rest was expected.

This experiment convinced the researchers in Budapest that the loud rest effect was a reliable phenomenon against which other variables could be measured. So now, at long last, we could begin on a real listening experiment with babies. All communication took place over the Internet. We exchanged many e-mails before setting up the first, pilot experiment.

I must say that I was shocked momentarily when I saw the first images. A sleeping baby with all sorts of electrodes stuck to its head. Was this acceptable? Fortunately, our colleagues in Budapest could put us at our ease: the baby slept through the sound presentation peacefully (see Figure 7.4).

The fourteen babies who took part in the experiment proper were all born in hospital, not because there was anything wrong with them, but because in Hungary it is customary to do so. Testing hearing is part of the standard care, and for our purposes, the test for beat induction was simply added on to all the other

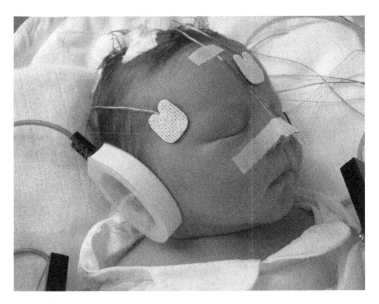

Figure 7.4 A two-day-old baby listening with headphones and four electrodes to measure its brain activity. The electrode on the nose was used as a reference. A parent was present throughout the listening experiment.

tests. A number of electrodes were stuck onto the babies' heads, together with a self-adhesive headphone. To ensure that the babies were at ease, their mothers fed them before the experiment began. Most then slept soundly during the listening experiment with their father or mother overseeing the whole procedure.

The EEG revealed that the sleeping babies' brains reacted in a similar way to those of the adults who listened to exactly the same rhythms; after a short while, an MMN could be seen, indicating that the (loud) rest was just where they had expected to hear a note. Here was evidence that even two or three-day-old babies noticed the (missing) beat in the music.

From this result, we could conclude that beat induction is an inborn cognitive skill with an apparently important biological function. Otherwise, what advantage would there be for a baby in being continually surprised with the omission of a beat in a variable rhythm? This suggests that the brains of newly born babies are completely ready for musical rhythms.

Nevertheless, contrary to the popular media that dispersed this news far and wide, we must interpret these results with care. Babies are able to hear sound three months before birth. While their brain development is ongoing, it is difficult to say whether a skill is inborn and "turned on" at a certain moment, or whether it has been acquired. Of these, the first seems to be the most plausible, because babies have an active sense of rhythm immediately after birth.

Assuming that this is indeed the case, the chance that cradling and dancing will have a fundamental influence on the sense of rhythm of babies (as was always supposed) becomes rather less probable. Without a doubt, these activities must strengthen or further develop a sensitivity to rhythm, but the rudimentary quality is already clearly present directly after birth.

We know a number of things about the effect of exposure to music before birth. For instance, newly born babies recognize the music that they have heard played during their stay in the womb. Newly born babies can also differentiate their mother's voice from the voices of other mothers, something which they must have learnt before birth.

However, it is one thing to recognize a voice or a certain piece of music, but quite another to be able to recognize a particular beat. The first can be explained as a product of *auditory memory*: a memory that stores specific sound patterns, with which newly heard sounds can be compared. Beat induction, however, is a cognitive mechanism on a higher, more abstract level; the beat has to be actively constructed (or inferred) from the music. There is a continuing effort to identify the neural mechanisms that underly beat induction, a topic that remains on the international research agenda.

LISTENING TO THE HEARTBEAT

What has been said above does not eliminate the fact that non-cognitive processes could also contribute to the capacity of beat induction. What effect does the heartbeat and other body rhythms, such as breathing and walking, have on developing a beat induction? Couldn't the mother's heartbeat before a baby is born provide a simple explanation for the presence of a sensitivity for the beat? After all, that is one of the sounds that they could listen to in the womb.

Unfortunately, it is not as simple as that. There are rather a lot of arguments against the heartbeat hypothesis. In the first place, recognizing periodic regularity is useful for many things, including recognizing heartbeats and possible irregularities in them. But, as was stated earlier, beat induction is a much more general and abstract form of this cognitive skill. It organizes our temporal expectations, so that silence at one place in a rhythm is noticeable, but not at another. For detecting a heartbeat, this sort of mechanism is unnecessary.

Secondly, there are many kinds of rhythmical sounds to listen to in the mother's body and in her surroundings. It is not justifiable, therefore, to ascribe the sense of rhythm in babies to just one sound, such as the mother's heartbeat.

Thirdly, we must not forget that other mammals have a heartbeat too. That ought to mean that our nearest relatives in the animal kingdom, such as apes and monkeys, should also be sensitive to the beat, simply because they too have been exposed to their mother's heartbeat. However, recent research suggests that beat induction is absent in monkeys. It seems that specific neural networks are needed to allow for beat induction, and that these networks are weaker or absent in apes and monkeys (see Further reading for recent developments).

Another link that is often made in scientific literature is the one between walking tempo and the tempo of music. Just as with the heartbeat hypothesis, many people find this idea attractive too: what we hear as being slow is comparable with walking slowly, what sounds fast seems to be in accordance with our running speed.

If you want to test this last hypothesis, then first of all you need to research what it is in our body that determines our walking tempo. However, there appears to be no inbuilt determining factor and body build bears no demonstrable relation to walking speed.

This didn't dissuade British bio-musicologist Neil Todd and his colleagues from researching whether body build had any influence on how tempo in music—the speed of the pulse or beat—was observed. Their hypothesis was that leg length influenced people's preference for a certain tempo. Expressed another way: people with short legs should prefer faster tempos. And that was indeed what the results—partly—showed. However, the researchers found no significant difference between women and men, although men, on average, have longer legs than women. All in all, the supposed connection between perception (the preferred tempo) and action (the walking tempo) strikes me as unconvincing.

Much more convincing is an experiment carried out by the North American music researchers Jessica Phillips-Silver and Laurel J. Trainor. They asked mothers to cradle their seven-month-old children in time to a rhythm that could be heard in two different ways: in 2/4 time (as in a march) or in 3/4 time (as in a waltz). Half of the babies were swung bounced up and down on every second beat of the bar; the other half on every third beat. By the end of the experiment, the researchers could show that the babies in the first group preferred rhythms with accents on every second beat (2/4 time), while the group that was cradled to a three-beat tune had a preference for rhythms with an accent on every third beat (3/4 time).[2] Thus, in a surprisingly simple experiment, it could be shown that movement indeed influences the perception of rhythm.

A DANCING COCKATOO

So there is a lot to say in favour of the idea that beat induction is an inborn skill. Assuming that a sense of regularity played a funda-mental role in the origins of music, and assuming (at least for the time being) that it is a unique human function, this implies that other animal species do *not* have a sense of rhythm at all.

In recent years, more and more research has been done on this point, and so far it seems as though this hypothesis is correct (contrary to Darwin's assumption; see Box 6.1). Until now, it has not been convincingly shown that apes or monkeys can clap or dance in time to music. They are very good at moving rhythmically, clapping, or beating themselves on the chest, as every visitor to the zoo knows. However, they have never been seen to do this synchronically with sound or music.

The big exception appears to be Snowball, the dancing cockatoo, that several years ago became a celebrity on the Internet. If you do not already know Snowball, this is the moment to look up a video on the Internet. You will see a white Cockatoo dancing, obviously with great pleasure, to the music of the Backstreet Boys and Queen, his favourite music. Snowball made several TV appearances, such as *The Late Show* of David Letterman. In addition, of course, the bird attracted the attention of researchers working on music cognition.

Was this an exception? Could this cockatoo hear the beat in the music and then move in time to it? Or was it imitating its owner? If you look at the first five seconds of the original YouTube video from 2007, then you see the shadow on the wall, of the dancing owner of the bird. You even get the impression that she has stuck a feather in her hair, which she sways enthusiastically backwards and forwards in time to the music, encouraging the bird to do the same. It seems, therefore, as though the bird is just imitating her, and, as we have known for a long time, cockatoos can do that very well.

Music researcher Ani Patel and his colleagues decided to put this phenomenon to the test. They designed an experiment in which the cockatoo was given three different versions of its favourite Backstreet Boys number to listen to; versions where the tempo had been sped up or slowed down, without that influencing the rest of the music (the pitch or the *timbre*). Their expectation was that if the cockatoo was really listening, then it would dance faster to one of the sped-up versions.

The available videos are convincing. Although Snowball didn't always move up and down in time to the music, in general it appeared to do it better, and certainly with more enthusiasm, than the average disco visitor.

While Snowball danced in synchrony with the music in only a small part of the video shots (between 5 and 20 percent of them), more and more studies suggest that cockatoos, and related species such as budgerigars, share something with us that we do not share with other apes or monkeys. It made Snowball an ambassador of a new field of research interested in revealing the *origins of musicality* (see Further reading).

This finding encouraged a lot of new research. Cognitive psychologist Adena Schachner and her research group analysed hundreds of Internet videos of animals moving or dancing to music. They managed convincingly to suggest that it is only species in the parrot and cockatoo families that have beat induction. Statistically, this is less strong, because for each animal, only one short film was available. But it did confirm the conjecture that something special was going on with parrots and cockatoos.

The question remains as to why something can be possible in cockatoos and parrots that, so far, has failed with chimpanzees and bonobos. Patel thinks that there is a direct relation between the ability to imitate speech and beat induction. The implication of his *vocal learning hypothesis* is that all songbirds have a sense of beat, or can learn it, at least. A number of research groups have now put this hypothesis on their agenda for testing (See Further reading).

Apart from all this, both the baby and the cockatoo research are nice examples of the impact that a new and unexpected empirical fact can have for trends of thought within a certain subject area. Compare this with a newly discovered fossil that has thrown out more than one existing theory about the course of evolution. Both theory and empiricism are also essential in music research in order to unravel and demystify the enigmas that it possesses.

BOX 7.1 ORIGINS OF BEAT INDUCTION

The topic of beat induction and being able to synchronize to music has attracted much attention in the last decade. Researchers from fields ranging from musicology to psychology and biology to neuroscience use the phenomenon to study how far the human brain is special, or whether beat induction has a long evolutionary history. Why can horses, dog and cats not move (spontaneously) in sync with the music, and can humans and cockatoos do it with so little effort?

The most recent member of the evolving animal orchestra is Ronan, a Californian sea lion. She was trained to bob her head in time to music, and not only appears to have better beat perception and synchronization than many people, but she is also challenging researchers' notions about beat induction in animals. Since sea lions are not known as *vocal learners*, the fact that Ronan can perceive and synchronize to the beat is refuting the *vocal learning hypothesis* (see main text). Again, the question remains: What do we, humans, share with cockatoos, and now sea lions, that we do not share with monkeys?

SUMMARY

To most of us it's very hard not to move to a beat; we seem to pick it up automatically. While not so long ago most theories considered *beat induction* a learned skill, acquired by repeatedly linking music and movement, a recent study in newborns showed that beat induction is an inborn skill. And since the rise of Snowball, the dancing cockatoo, more animals have proved they are also able to move to the beat. Strangely, no other primates (beside humans) as yet.

NOTES

1 In Chapter 10, we will see that music theory assumes that listeners will hear a "loud rest" if a note is omitted on the expected beat, such as on the first beat of the bar—the *downbeat*. Also the notions of "syncopation" and "metric tree" will be explained there in further detail.
2 Phillips-Silver and Trainor could substantiate their findings by using the head-turn preference paradigm. This is a method by which the time taken by a baby to show an interest in something by turning its head in a certain direction—in this case, towards a loudspeaker presenting some particular music or rhythm—is used as a standard measurement.

FURTHER READING

Honing, H. (2019). *The Evolving Animal Orchestra. In Search of What Makes Us Musical.* Cambridge, MA: The MIT Press.
Honing, H. (Ed.). (2018). *The Origins of Musicality.* Cambridge, MA: The MIT Press.

Patel, A. D., Iversen, J. R., Bregman, M. R., & Schulz, I. (2009). "Experimental evidence for synchronization to a musical beat in a nonhuman animal." *Current Biology*, 19, 827–830.

Winkler, I., Haden, G., Ladinig, O., Sziller, I., & Honing, H. (2009). "Newborn infants detect the beat in music." *Proceedings of the National Academy of Sciences*, 106, 2468–2471.

DO YOU RECOGNIZE THIS MELODY?

Do you have perfect pitch? Why is relative pitch more special than absolute pitch?

We have seen that beat induction is essential for hearing and appreciating a rhythm. But can the same be said of a melody? In other words, is there a comparable, cognitive function for the melodic dimension of musicality? What makes it possible to hear and appreciate a melody, and what are the underlying requirements? Is there a pitch-related cognitive skill that is music-specific, inborn, and unique to human beings?

If you ask musicians to give an example of an exceptional musical listening skill, then the first thing that many of them think of is "absolute pitch." Someone who has absolute or "perfect" pitch can name a piano note, without seeing which piano key has been played. Students at a music academy would particularly love to have this gift, because that would make it much easier for them to do the musical dictations—writing down in musical notation what the teacher plays or sings—which they are often given as exercises.

Contrary to what the term suggests, absolute pitch is not so much a hearing skill as it is a cognitive skill. You must be able to remember and name a certain note, and also to classify sequences of notes which have very different *timbres* (such as those produced by a piano, violin, or voice) into a certain category.

You can compare the skill with naming colors. Just as each color is physically determined by a certain frequency of light (for example, blue has a higher frequency than red), so is the pitch of every note determined by a specific sound frequency. Musicians call a note of 440 Hz (440 vibrations per second) an A, and one of approximately

DOI: 10.4324/9781003158301-11

494 Hz, a B. However, the strange thing here is that almost all of us can name colors easily, but when it comes to pitch, only a few people seem to have this capacity.

To have perfect pitch is a valuable, rare gift that many musicians try to acquire for practical reasons. For instance, it is extremely handy if you can sing or play the correct notes immediately from the sheet music. However, people who claim to have absolute or perfect pitch are often faced with a serious problem. They complain that, "I can't hear melodies, I only hear the names of notes passing by." Perfect pitch sounds like a musical magic potion, but in practice you are more likely to have problems with it because, very often, it leads to an unmusical way of listening.

ABSOLUTE PITCH

For a long time, absolute pitch was mainly seen as the outcome of a genetically determined gift: you were born with it. But although there is clear evidence that absolute pitch has a genetic component, it seems for a large part the result of exposure to music at an early age followed by intensive musical training. For example, in a country such as Japan, perfect pitch occurs much more frequently than elsewhere (among music academy students, the percentage is sometimes as high as 70 percent). This could be explained by the fact that Japan is a country where music is an important part of the education of young children, who are strongly encouraged to play music at an early stage.

Some idiosyncrasies of people with absolute pitch also indicate that this skill must have been learned (or at least modified by learning). In an experiment, mistakes in naming notes were elicited sooner by naming notes played on the black keys of a piano than on the white ones. And this even though, for the sound, it makes no difference whether white or black keys were used! The only plausible explanation that can be thought of for this is that, to develop absolute pitch, knowledge of the piano keyboard must have been a contributory factor.

Finally, the outcomes of studies on absolute pitch are quite strongly influenced by the manner in which this phenomenon is researched. You can ask yourself, how realistic is it to ask someone to name a single note, or to use fragments of music that are unfamiliar to some of the people taking part in the experiment. This is why, nowadays, music researchers design experiments in which both musicians and non-musicians can take part, and use musical material that people know from their own environment. The surprising thing is that, then, absolute pitch suddenly appears to be a much more widespread skill.

A beautiful example is the research carried out by the music psychologist Glenn Schellenberg, mentioned earlier (see Chapter 1, p. 10), at the University of Toronto. The method involved asking about fifty students to listen to the opening tunes of well-known television programs. According to the students, none of them had absolute pitch. In the experiment they heard two versions of each tune: one was the original and the other was pitched whole tone higher or lower, using a computer program.

The students were then asked to indicate which version of the tune was the original one that they knew from the TV program. According to a probability calculation, if they were to guess, then an average of 50 percent of the answers would be correct. However, the students gave the correct answer in 70 percent of the cases!

When, recently, I gave an informal demonstration inspired by this research for children aged between eight and twelve years, more than 80 percent of them gave the correct answer for opening tunes of popular TV programs for children, such as Sesame Street. Conclusion: absolute memory for pitch seems quite widespread.

Another example comes from a study by Dan Levitin, who, at the time, was affiliated with Stanford University. He asked students to choose their favourite CD out of a range of CDs, to think of a certain song, and then to sing it (without having first listened to it).

Although the problem with these sorts of assignment is that you don't know which mistakes were caused by singing the tune and which originated from listening to it at an earlier date; of all the participants (none of them professional singers), up to two-thirds were no more than a tone off. Obviously, we all have a good, so-called "echoic memory" for music; comparable with a photographic memory for images— especially for songs which we hear frequently in a certain version.

You can easily test this yourself. Think of a well-known song, such as *Stayin' Alive* from the Bee Gees, and then sing it aloud, if necessary, in the bathroom or in the shed. It's very likely that both the tempo and the pitch will match the original.

By the way, *Stayin' Alive* was recommended by North-American heart specialists as being an ideal support for the memory, in that it has exactly the right tempo for giving cardiopulmonary resuscitation (CPR) after someone has had a heart attack. So, music can sometimes even save lives!

The question remains of whether absolute pitch is a necessary condition for perceiving melody, a capability unique to human beings. Absolute pitch seems to be an inborn talent, because even young children can recognize basic differences in pitch (i.e., the difference between low vs. middle vs. high tones, even when taken out of context). Most of us apparently lose the skill because it is not very useful. Others, who have musical instruments around, keep the skill active. But, nevertheless, it is not this that makes us different from other creatures, such as songbirds, wolves, and ferrets. They, too, all have absolute pitch! So, in fact, this skill is quite widespread; it's nothing special, and there is much to be said for the opinion that it has little, if anything to do with musicality.

RELATIVE PITCH

What then is special about being able to recognize a melody? *Relative* pitch. Just as with rhythm, it seems that, for melody, absolute pitch is not exceptional at all. In fact, it's quite ordinary. While a closer look at something that we do consider very ordinary—relative pitch—shows this to be *really* exceptional.

Relative pitch is the capacity to recognize a melody that does not necessarily have the same absolute pitches. When you hear the first notes of *Twinkle, Twinkle Little Star*, you will immediately recognize the nursery rhyme, whether it's sung high or low. What we recognize is the structure of the melody and the relative distance between the pitches of the notes: a few steps up or down and so on. We recognize a melody mainly from its "contour" (the changes in pitch) and not from the individual absolute pitches (the frequencies), even though we may have already heard those before in the same sequence. We make abstractions from melodies that we've heard before.

When the first note of *Twinkle, Twinkle Little Star* is sung, if the first tone is played at 400 Hz, that produces a totally different version than when the first tone is played at 500 Hz. This applies both to the frequencies of the vibrations and to the absolute distance between those frequencies. Nevertheless, we hear the same melody each time. This phenomenon, known as *perceptual invariance*, is present in all sorts of attributes and modalities of human perception: in speech, for example, but also in sight and in voluntary movements. A famous example is recognizing geometrical objects such as those shown in Figure 8.1.

All the objects in this figure are easy to recognize as being the same object, whether they are turned around, moved, or made larger or smaller. Even though all sorts of measurable, physical aspects of that object change, we recognize all the variations in that picture as being the same object. Relative pitch is something similar. Whether a melody is played somewhat higher or lower, we nevertheless recognize it as being the same tune.

That may seem obvious, but what we encounter here is an exceptional function of our perceptual system. It is a music-specific function, disassociated more or less completely from language,

Figure 8.1 Are all the objects the same?

which develops spontaneously and is unique to human beings. In short, it is a function that must have played an important role in helping human beings to create music in the first place. I have been able to demonstrate something similar with respect to beat induction, which appears to be an inborn human skill, in the sense that we could establish that beat induction is a cognitive mechanism that is active from our birth onwards. Can we make a similar case for relative pitch?

It's an intriguing question, and the answer—"yes"—is equally intriguing. Developmental psychologists have shown that the aptitude for both absolute and relative pitch is present in all babies. However, by the time they're a few months old, a hierarchy in these capacities emerges and babies gradually attend more to the relative aspects of a melody than to the absolute, actual pitch of the notes. Relative pitch supersedes absolute pitch as it were.

Moreover, the (few) experiments that have only been carried out on animals so far, show, without exception, that animals have no relative pitch at all, only absolute pitch. Research on rhesus monkeys showed that they only recognized melodies if they heard them at exactly the same pitch or if they were played at one or more octaves higher or lower than before. A melody that was played only a few tones higher or lower was not recognized as being similar. Songbirds, too, only have absolute pitch. For them, apparently a melody sung a fraction higher or lower is a completely different melody: it's considered another bird!

Why is relative pitch so important? And why should we be happy that we have it? Apart from the fact that relative pitch enables us to recognize melodies without being influenced by their absolute pitch, this talent is also extremely helpful in recognizing many other variants. The analogy with beat induction comes to the fore again: for that, too, a more abstract way of listening is required. Thanks to relative pitch, we are able not only to recognize two melodies as one and the same tune, but we can also identify the one melody as being a variant of the other.

How we, as human beings, do that precisely is still unclear. But the analogy with having a sense of rhythm again offers the necessary stable point for comparison. Just as the beat (or meter) is important for interpreting rhythm, so is harmony (also referred to as *tonality*) important for interpreting a melody. Both of them are mental constructions that we use for interpreting music. A feel for rhythmic regularities and harmony lend structure to our listening experience. We use these two constructions as bases from which to project our expectations about music. And thanks to that same sense of rhythm and harmony, we are able to hear the same melody in very different ways.

BOX 8.1 ABSOLUTE AND RELATIVE PITCH

- *Absolute pitch* (also referred to as *perfect pitch*) is the rare ability of a person to identify or recreate a given musical note without the benefit of a reference tone. Absolute pitch may be demonstrated naming a note (is it an A or a G?) or reproducing a heard tone on a musical instrument. Absolute pitch is quite common in the animal world (search for "dog perfect pitch" on the Internet to see an intriguing example).
- *Relative pitch* is the ability to recognize a melody regardless of the exact pitch (register) or tempo at which it is heard or sung. Most people listen not to a melody's individual tones and their frequencies but to the melody as a whole. Whether you hear "Mary Had a Little Lamb" sung at a higher or lower pitch, you still recognize the song. But note that relative pitch in humans can mean more than just hearing relationships between pitches. Familiar melodies in which the pitch is rendered unrecognizable, for example, can also be identified from the contours of other aspects of sound.

SUMMARY

Absolute pitch appears to be more widespread than thought before. In several studies, children and grown-ups appeared to have some form of absolute pitch—as do songbirds, wolves, and ferrets. Relative pitch is a different thing. All humans have it, most animals don't. It's a music-specific function that might have played an important role in the evolutionary origins of our capacity for music.

FURTHER READING

Jacoby, N., Undurraga, E. A., McPherson, M. J., Valdés, J., Ossandón, T., & McDermott, J. H. (2019). "Universal and non-universal features of musical pitch perception revealed by singing." *Current Biology*, 29 (19), 3229–3243.

Oxenham, A. J. (2019). "Pitch: perception and neural coding." In P. J. Rentfrow & D. Levitin (Eds.), *Foundations in Music Psychology: Theory and Research* (pp. 3–32). Cambridge, MA: The MIT Press.

Russo, F. A. (2019). "Pitch combinations and grouping." In P. J. Rentfrow & D. Levitin (Eds.), *Foundations in Music Psychology: Theory and Research* (pp. 121–148). Cambridge, MA: The MIT Press.

PART 4

TÁ-TA-TA-TÁ-TA:
MUSIC AS COGNITION

THE SECRET OF THE "LOUD REST"

What is musical listening about? What makes music exciting? Could music theory help us to understand our listening experience?

Now that I have talked at length about what is not music—that it's neither sound, nor language—it's high time that I tell you what music actually is. In this chapter, with the help of two fully worked out examples, I will show that music always takes place in the listener's mind, whether in the plush seating of a concert hall, in an easy chair at home, or in a reverberating stadium. Music is cognition. It is not the components of music as such, but the listener's overall perception, expectation, and memory of them that transforms those components into a pleasurable listening experience—into music.

Apart from being a pleasure, music can also be exciting. This applies especially to the rhythm, in that the pauses or rests between the sounds play just as important a role as the sounds themselves. What is the secret of these "loud rests"?

Below, is the notation of a very well-known rhythm (one we have seen before in Figure 4.1). In the same way as reading the words of a sentence, we read this notation from left to right: a vertical line represents a *strike* on a drum or a tick with a pen on a table. A small square represents a *rest*, a tap in the air. Had the vertical lines been embossed—as in braille—then you would have been able to hear the rhythm by moving a plastic teaspoon along the paper from left to right, slowly and evenly stroking the lines.

This rhythm is a seven-note cadence that we often hear around us. It often comes combined with the text "*Shave and a haircut,*" a short pause, and then, sung with great emphasis, a rowdy "*two bits!*" It doesn't seem to lose its attraction to hooting motorists.

DOI: 10.4324/9781003158301-13

Figure 9.1 The rhythm of "Shave and a haircut" notated with bars and dots.

There are many other variants in circulation and in many languages. In addition, you come across it in various pop songs, jazz numbers, cartoon films, and musicals. Obviously, there is something widely attractive and catchy about this rhythm.

Without a doubt, this is an example of a "rhythmical cliché." After a few notes, most people would recognize this rhythm, and if, after five beats, it was discontinued, then they would have the inclination to complete the cadence. This effect would probably be even stronger if the melody was also included (shown in Figure 4.1). Listeners would then feel almost *compelled* to complete it.

Try this out sometime with a group of friends or acquaintances. Whistle the first five notes and then put your index finger over your lips to indicate "quiet, please!" I can guarantee that one or two people in your audience will spontaneously whistle aloud the remaining part of the melody, or that most of the people listening, if not everyone, will hear the last two notes loud and clear in their heads, as though each head was functioning as a concert hall!

This shows, for example, that listening is not just a passive activity. Already after a few notes, we can almost guess what we are going to hear, and if the tune ends abruptly, then we fill in the missing notes. Both situations are proof that we are actively listening along with the music. So it's not the "tone" that make the music—*C'est le ton qui fait la musique* … —but the listener.

A VERY PRONOUNCED NOTHING

In addition to the compelling inherent urge to complete the melody, this cliché contains something that music theorists call a "loud rest." The majority of listeners will expect to hear a note just after the fifth beat—namely, a note that coincides with the second of the three small squares.

Figure 9.2 The same rhythm as in Figure 9.1, but now with one of the dots marked.

But that note doesn't come … The grey oblong indicates a silence, one that, unlike the other rests (shown by small squares), doesn't pass unnoticed. This silence is obtrusive, hence the term "loud rest": it is a very pronounced nothing.

It is this palpable quietness that makes the rhythm exciting, even though it is a cliché. It doesn't matter how often you have heard it, and even though you know for sure that the one note will be left out, it continues to sound exciting. No matter how hard you try, you can't hear it in any other way. This is generally a sign that our consciousness has temporarily lost its power over our listening capacities.

Such a listening experience can be compared with the well-known visual illusion, shown in Figure 9.3. Although we know that both horizontal lines are equally long, our perception continues to tell us that the uppermost line is longer. Nevertheless, if you check it, you will find that both lines are the same length. Our perception, in this case, rejects what our brains already know. For a moment we are both deaf and blind: immune to mental processes governed by our short or long-term memories.

It is this effect that lies behind the element of tension or excitement in rhythmical clichés. Even though every loud rest incites a

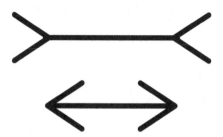

Figure 9.3 The Müller-Lyer illusion.

strong expectation that fails to materialize, that sort of experience seems not to be stored in our memories. On the next occasion, the expected moment will be just as unexpected as it was before. In the same way, a familiar but long-deferred punch line of a joke never fails to take people by surprise.

WHAT MAKES A REST "LOUD?"

To be able to test whether the surprise in a rhythm is, indeed, caused by one specific "silent" moment in time, all we need to do is to change one note in the rhythm. For example, if we exchange the position of the loud rest with the note that follows it, or, to put it differently, move the next to the last note to the position of the loud rest, then the whole effect of a loud rest is lost.

The above rhythm sounds like a boring march—a rhythm that one quickly forgets.

What makes this rhythm so different from the rhythmical cliché? Why do we hear a loud rest in the latter at the place where the arrow begins, but not in the rhythm above? After all, physically, the rest in the march is exactly the same as the one in the cliché: it is three small squares in length, so it is just as long as the loud rest in the rhythmical cliché.

The explanation can largely be found in the cognitive process called "beat induction" that was introduced before: the well-known phenomenon that we often hear a regular pulse while listening to a piece of music or to a rhythm such as the one above, even though not every beat is explicitly present, nor do they have to be. Anyone who hears a piece of music usually has no difficulty at all in clapping to the regular pulse or *beat*. If the music goes faster, then the person hears that and claps faster, staying in time with the music; and precisely the opposite will happen if the tempo is reduced.

Figure 9.4 Rhythm example.

Most people can easily move a finger or a foot in time to the music. However, it should be noted that very many rhythms do not explicitly have a regular beat. Look, for example, at the rhythm below.

Several regularities can be distinguished here. But listeners only hear one or two of them. The majority of listeners would hear beats at the locations corresponding to the dots given in Figure 9.6.

However, the accents that occur at regular intervals from each other are not part of the rhythm itself, because, by definition, each note sounds exactly the same. The regular pulse is evoked (*induced*) by the rhythm, hence the term "induction." It is the listener who adds the regular beat to the rhythm.

We also superimpose this regular system of accents onto even the simplest rhythms. For example, think of the sound of a ticking clock. It is a rhythm that everyone in the first instance would note down as a simple series of stripes, where the distance between every tick is exactly the same: an isochronous rhythm. What we hear, however, is not an isochronous series of ticks, "tick-tick-tick-tick," but a regular, "tick-tock-tick-tock." Here, too, the listener superimposes extra information onto the rhythm, thus creating a system of accents that

Figure 9.5 A beat inducing rhythm

Figure 9.6 The same rhythm as shown in Figure 9.5, but now with dots underneath.

makes some ticks more important and more noticeable than others even though, physically, they are identical.

Compare this with perspective in a painting. Usually, the perspective is not really visible; there are no lines, all going to the same vanishing point, drawn over the painted images. Nonetheless, we see depth in the painting. And that's why two figures in a painting may appear to differ in size, even though, in centimeters, they are exactly the same.

Beat induction is a comparable phenomenon. When listening to a rhythm, we project a temporal regularity onto it that superimposes a pattern of accents so that some locations gain more emphasis than others.

It is this regularity, created by the listener, that explains the loud rest in the rhythmical cliché. After the first four or five notes, we already hear a pulse or the beat (see the illustration below, with the beats indicated by dots.)

Figure 9.7 Pen drawing showing two trees, a person, two trees and another person in perspective.

Figure 9.8 A rhythm identical to that in figure 9.1, but now with the beat marked with dots underneath the pattern.

At these indicated positions, we expect to hear a note that will confirm the "imagined" beat or regular pulse. However, in the case of the cliché, that note is *missing* so, consequently, without realizing it, we create "an empty moment" that reveals itself to us as a loud rest. If you think about it, it's a paradoxical process: the rhythm violates, as it were, the expectations that it has itself created.

The (mental) activity that a listener undertakes in superimposing a regular pulse to a rhythm is typically a "bottom-up" process. The latter term indicates how a listener adds structure to the unstructured material offered. In contrast, the way in which a beat is induced, and consequently structures the act of listening, is identifiable as a "top-down" process. This indicates that the listener uses (implicit) knowledge to interpret unstructured rhythms. In other words: what someone hears influences what he knows, and what someone knows influences what he hears. It is a dynamic process in which first, while listening, an expectation is built up, that then influences what is heard thereafter.

It remains a great challenge for cognitive scientists to capture this process in exact, formal terms. It means that scientists are trying to formulate their theory in precise enough terms to enable them to feed their information into a computer. If they succeed, then, for each rhythm, the computer program will show which regular pulse is predicted for that specific rhythm.

Within the area of investigation discussed here, this aspiration is not yet an actuality: the programs that have been developed so far are unable, as yet, to find the beat in a wide range of rhythmical examples. Our knowledge of rhythms—and of listeners worldwide—is still not advanced enough (see Further reading).

Many composers seem to know exactly how to manipulate the expectations of their audiences. If their use of rhythm arouses too few expectations, then their classical composition or song will very quickly be found boring. If, on the other hand, they arouse too many expectations, then the listener will receive too many signals and the rhythm will rapidly become incomprehensible to them. So, it's all about finding the correct balance between the two: inducing a regular pulse, yet breaking the expectations. It is a quest that has resulted in the creation of some fantastic rhythms ranging from the samba to the calypso, and from the salsa to the bossa nova, all of which are far more complex rhythms than the rhythmical cliché. But they are all based on the same cognitive mechanism—beat induction; or, in everyday English—a sense of rhythmic regularity.

WILL THE SECRET BE DISCLOSED?

Although the secret of the loud rest has not yet been completely disclosed, we have discovered, meanwhile, which factors cause an exciting rhythm. However, a description is not the same as an explanation. Which are the exciting rhythms and which are not, and why? What makes one rhythm more exciting than another? Which rhythm is the most exciting?

To be able to answer these, and similar questions, we need a quantitative model that can calculate how loud a "loud rest" is. To begin with, we need to realize that there is sometimes more structure in a pattern of accents than just a single pulse. We hear "tick-tock tick-tock," for instance, rather than "tick-tock-tock tick-tock-tock." In this second case, we hear an additional accent (the tick's) on every third beat (as in a waltz): "tick-tock-tock tick-tock-tock"; while, in the first case, we hear an additional accent on every second beat (as in a march): "tick-tock tick-tock." This metrical structure or meter need be nothing more than two or more levels of pulse. Here it is comprised of the perceived pulse that you can tap to with your foot, the beat-level or tactus, plus the level at which this beat forms clusters of two or three beats (duple or triple meter), as described above. The latter, the bar-level, forms a slower pulse that emphasizes some positions in the tactus more than others, thereby creating a hierarchical structure. One can also have additional layers above the measure and/ or below the tactus (indeed, it is common to have the tactus divided into rapid duplets, triplets, or quadruplets). These two or more levels of hierarchy can be visualized with the help of a "metrical tree": a structure comparable to the syntactical trees used in linguistics.

A metrical tree, such as the one shown above, illustrates a unit that we call a "measure" or "bar." It branches upwards and each time it divides, it produces two or three new branches. The longer the vertical branch is, the stronger the emphasis at that point in the music. And that emphasis is expressed as a number that quantifies what the emphasis for each position in the rhythm, as experienced by the listener, actually is.[1]

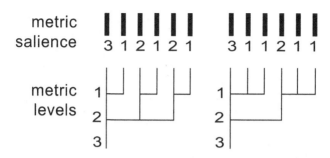

Figure 9.9 An isochronous rhythm, with below it a metrical tree

This perhaps seems complicated, but if we look at the two examples above, then, actually, it's very simple. We can hear one and the same rhythm in various ways: in twos (the example on the left), but also in threes (the example on the right), or all sorts of combinations of them. Most Western listeners, however, have the tendency to prefer listening to rhythms that are split into groups of two beats rather than clusters of three. This is probably because duple meter occurs more frequently in our culture than triple meter. However, such a duple bias may also have a neurological basis, as is suggested by some recent brain imaging studies.

CALCULATING THE LOUDNESS OF RESTS

In music theory a loud rest is sometimes called a "syncope," a term that literally means a "joined beat." Therefore, a "syncope" indicates not so much how something is heard, but more the way in which it's written down. It is notated as a slur between two notes to indicate that those two notes should be played as a single one. (NB: If played on a percussion instrument, this would sound exactly like Figure 9.1.)

Figure 9.10 The rhythm of "Shave and a haircut" notated in 2/4 using Western musical notation.

Most music encyclopedias describe a syncope as "an accent that has been moved forward," and "to syncopate" as "a technique often used by composers to avoid regularity in rhythm by displacing an emphasis in that rhythm." Although these appear to be clear definitions, they don't describe the technique or the outcome sufficiently: for instance, not all shifted accents are syncopes (for example, the offbeat accompaniment that is common in reggae and ska). Moreover, these definitions do not explain why the one rhythm can sound more syncopated than the other. Moreover, these definitions say nothing about what the listener actually hears. For that one needs a cognitive model.

One of the first researchers to try to define the exact difference between syncopes, from the perspective of the listener, was Christopher Longuet-Higgins (mentioned briefly in the previous chapter). He provided a formal definition that allows one to calculate whether a note (or a rest) is accented (or "loud"), and to what extent.

Below, I include the rhythmical cliché again, and under that, a metrical tree that represents duple meter.

Given this information, one can calculate the "loudness" of the rest by subtracting the numerical value of the salience of the note

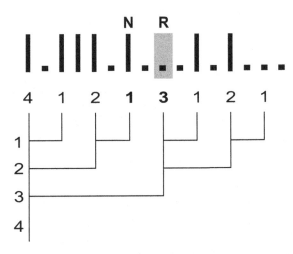

Figure 9.11 The rhythm of "Shave and a haircut" (as Figure 9.8) with underneath it a metrical tree: a duple meter.

preceding that rest (represented by a letter N) from the rest itself (represented by a letter R). In the above example: $N - R = 1 - 3 = -2$. The more negative the outcome of this calculation, the louder the rest. If we carry out the same procedure for the rhythm in which we had displaced a single note …

… then we can calculate that the rest there has a value of 2 ($N - R = 3 - 1 = 2$). The result then is positive, so there is no loud rest. By using the Longuet-Higgins model, therefore, we can very easily, and exactly, express the difference heard between two physically identical silences or rests.

By definition, the Longuet-Higgins model assumes that the strength of the loud rest depends on which meter is heard. However, the model does not calculate the meter itself, but assumes that it is known. If you also want to quantify that meter, then that will have to be calculated using a supplementary model (something Longuet-Higgins and others tried to do later on).

As a double-check, the reliability of the prediction produced by means of the Longuet-Higgins model can be tested by substituting the duple meter for a composite meter, a combination of duple and triple divisions.

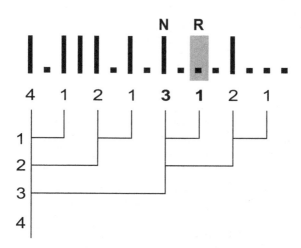

Figure 9.12 The rhythm of Figure 9.4 (without a "loud rest") with underneath it a metrical tree: a duple meter.

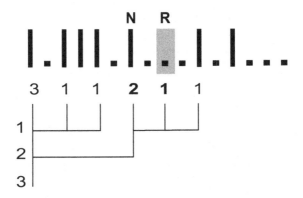

Figure 9.13 The rhythm of "Shave and a haircut" (as Figure 9.8) with underneath it a metrical tree: a triple meter.

And what emerges? If you were to hear the rhythmical cliché with this meter in mind (also called "6/8 time"), then the loud rest would disappear (N − R = 2 − 1 = 1). What the Longuet-Higgins model reveals here is that it is the listener who makes this rhythm exciting, by projecting a specific meter onto the music. If the listener has another expectation, and projects another regularity or metrical structure, then that person will experience the rhythm differently by, for instance, finding it boring instead of exciting.

MEASURING IS KNOWING

Although the Longuet-Higgins model is able to express in numbers our intuition about certain rhythms, this does not mean that it can teach us something about rhythms in general. For that, we need knowledge based on empirical experiments.

Longuet-Higgins himself preferred to base his theories and formalizations on his—mostly brilliant—intuitions and insights. It was left to Leigh M. Smith and Olivia Ladinig to experimentally test Longuet-Higgins' model. To test the model described above empirically, they compared the results of existing listening experiments with Longuet-Higgins' predictions. In spite of the simplicity of his model, he could explain the results for roughly three quarters of the data. That's quite something!

A LISTENING TEST

So far, I have concentrated in great length on the two factors that make rhythms exciting: the loud rest and the (active) role played by the listener. This does not mean, though, that everything has been said about the rhythmical cliché. Indeed, "measuring is knowing," but that is still only part of the story. Our perception also plays an important role—and that is far more difficult to measure. For instance, there is the interesting question of where—at what point in the rhythm—the excitement manifests itself the most clearly.

In this example, is note A the most salient? Or the rest, B? Or is it perhaps even the following note, C?

After all that has already been said, the tendency will be for you to choose B. But you might also have hesitated … Don't worry, you're in good company! Music theorists are also strongly divided over this issue.

Musicologist David Huron would predict, on the basis of what he calls *event-related binding*, that listeners will find note A the most exciting. The reasoning behind this is that listeners associate a certain quality in what they have experienced, such as "exciting" or "boring," with a happening (an event), and not with the moment in time when the event was expected to take place (in our case, during a rest). The exciting element about the rest is attributed to the note preceding it (the A), which then, retrospectively, sounds syncopated.

Longuet-Higgins' model gives no indication of whether either note (A) or rest (B), sounds syncopated. His model only predicts how loud a rest will sound, not whether it is A or B that creates the tension.

Music theorist Justin London, who first used the term "loud rest," would surely choose B.

Figure 9.14 The rhythm of "Shave and a haircut" (as Figure 9.8) with underneath it three letters: an "A" on the note just before the "loud rest", a "B" on the loud rest itself, and a "C" on the note just after it.

To my knowledge, there is no theory that points to C being the most salient moment. Having said that, it would be interesting to find out which prediction matches with what we, as listeners, actually hear. Only empirical data can offer an outcome and act as a neutral adjudicator. This is, once again, rather unusual in musicology—but it is quite common in the cognitive sciences of music, and in this case, it is relatively easy to test.

During the writing of this text we did an informal experiment on the Internet (see www.amsterdammusiclab.nl) to which about 500 people responded. Of these, about 20 percent found A to be the most exciting, 60 percent B (the rest), and just under 20 percent C (the note following the rest).

It seems, therefore, that most people experience the loud rest as the most salient moment. However, the Internet experiment, as said before, was only a demonstration; we can't attach any general conclusions to it. However, a systematic listening experiment shows that the majority of people, whether they are musicians or not, do not notice the notes so much as the silences occurring at metrically accentuated moments. Or, in other words, while music may contain many silences (such as pauses between notes and phrases) we almost never notice them. When we *do* notice a silence, it is a very unusual moment—and hence highly salient.

MELODY AND EXPECTATION

In the example of the "Shave and a haircut" cliché, in addition to expectation, the fact that we have already heard the tune very often must also be taken into consideration; it is not called a cliché without reason. We have only to see or hear a fragment of it to be able to fill in the rest. As we said at the beginning of this chapter, that effect is even stronger if we not only hear the rhythm of the cliché, but also the melody.

Actually, the rhythmical cliché is, in all its compactness, a mini-composition. Its typical form, divided into an introduction, a development, and a cadence can be found in various full-scale compositions. Within the seven-note melody (C-G-G-A flat-G-... -B-C), we can view the first five notes as the introduction, and the last two as the closure. It is also possible to make an even more refined subdivision, with an introduction (the first note, C), a question (the two notes G and G), an answer (the notes A flat and G), and closure (the last two notes, B and C).

What is important here for my argument, is to note that, as listeners, we make use of *implicit* knowledge about the structure of music, without realizing it. The—hidden—musical rules ensure that we anticipate that particular notes or chords will be played sooner than others, whether we are familiar with the concepts of music theory—such as chord schemes and cadences—or not.

In this way, the tension in the melody of the rhythmical cliché that is resolved by the last two notes utilizes an implicit harmony: a typical sequence of chords that is found in a lot of Western music. It is a sort of template that can be reduced to two chords: the "*tonic*" and the "*dominant.*" The tonic is stable; for instance, you end a song with it. The dominant is unstable and requires "resolution." It needs closure in the form of the (implied) root or tonic.

If you cut off a song abruptly on the dominant, then everyone listening to it will get the feeling that the song is not finished. For instance, if you only sing the first seven notes of *Twinkle, twinkle little star*, everyone will hear the silence that follows: "Twinkle, twinkle little star …" The second phrase—"how I wonder what you are"—completes the ditty. Expressed in music-theory terms, it's the last note, the tonic, that provides *closure*.

Many listening experiments have been carried out that offer the possibility of finding out how this works, and whether the effect is dependent upon the culture in which the listener has grown up, and especially the person's musical preference at that time. I will go into this in detail in the following chapter, but for the time being, it's sufficient to say that we not only have an inborn sense of rhythm and melody, but also *acquire* expectations for specific structure and regularity by simply exposing ourselves to music.

We not only anticipate that a certain sequence of notes will be repeated, or that the melody will continue as we know it, but we also expect a paradigmatic structure on a more abstract level, such as a particular sequence of chords. The notes don't have to be exactly the same each time, but the framework, the more abstract (harmonic) characteristics *do*. In our Western music, that framework—and there I mean in classical music, pop, and jazz—consists of no more than three chords: three chords that can be found in the largest part of all songs and compositions.

When we listen to music, we extract regularity and structure out of it, whether we like it or not. In particular, we hear the chords that we, as listener, most expect, and also the chords that we frequently hear in a certain sequence. If we hear the first two chords from a frequently heard series of three in an unknown song, we will again expect to hear the third chord, after the first two.

The same thing happens, in fact, with the cliché: the first five notes evoke in the listener, without them realizing it, a classical tonic-dominant-tonic sequence. The result is that the listener *has* to hear the final C to get the feeling that the melody is complete and rounded off. This explains why, if someone else whistles the first five notes, most people will hear the last two notes in their heads.

In addition, in the melody C-G-G-A flat-G- ... -B-C, the B can be substituted by a G without consequence, because a B and a G both fit into the implicit framework of chords for the song, and will hardly interfere with the listener's expectation. If the B is substituted by a C sharp, a tone that does not fit into the implicit chord, then that will be immediately noticeable.

In short, even when it comes to a simple tune, it turns out that a Western listener not only takes an active part in structuring the rhythm, but, in fact, is also ready and able to use and apply the basic rules of Western harmony.

BOX 9.1 WHICH RHYTHM IS SYNCOPATED?

The interaction of rhythm and metrical structure, and the role that cognition plays in its perception and appreciation, can be illustrated with the phenomenon of *syncopation*. To illustrate this, consider the two rhythms depicted in Figure 9.15. Which of these is a syncopated rhythm?

A formally trained musician will easily point out the left example, guided by the slur marking a syncopation. However, as performed

Figure 9.15 The rhythm of "Shave and a haircut" in common music notation, notated in 2/4 on left and in 6/8 on the right.

by a drum computer, these notated rhythms will sound identical!
The reader here is influenced by the notation. When we listen to a
rhythm (even if it is simply a series of isochronous clicks, like a
clock), we tend to interpret it in a metrical fashion, and hear it as
syncopated, or not, depending on our metric expectations. A time
signature in the notation is no guarantee that a listener will perceive
the meter as such. This is illustrated by the example in Figure 9.16.

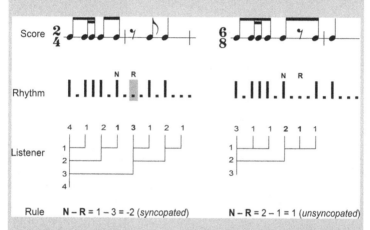

Figure 9.16 Two possible notations (labelled as "Score") of the same rhythm
(labelled as "Rhythm").

In the left example a metrical tree represents a duple meter; in the
right example it represents a compound meter (labelled as "Listener").
The numbers at the leaves of the metrical tree represent the theoretical
metric salience (the depth of the tree at that position in the rhythm). A
negative difference between the metric salience of a certain note N and
the succeeding rest R indicates a *syncopation* (according to Longuet-
Higgins' formal model; see p. 96–98). The more negative this difference, the more syncopated the note N and "louder" the rest R.

SUMMARY

Music listening is not just about the music on one end and the
listener on the other, it's about the interaction between the two,

with the listener's perception, memory, and expectations contributing in important ways. When music sounds exciting to us, it has the right balance of expected and unexpected events, and, like the "loud rest," is a result of the listener's expectations. Whether we are familiar with the concepts of music theory or not, our expectations are built on an implicit knowledge of music. So we do not only have an inborn sense of rhythm and melody, we also acquire rhythmic and melodic expectations simply by being exposed to music.

NOTE

1 In Western musical notation, a meter is usually indicated by two numbers placed at the beginning of the staff: in the example on the left, that would be "3/4" and on the right, "6/8" (see Box 9.1).

FURTHER READING

Honing, H. (2013). "Structure and interpretation of rhythm in music." In D. Deutsch (Ed.), *Psychology of Music*, 3rd edition (pp. 369–404). London, UK: Academic Press.

London, J. (2012). *Hearing in Time: Psychological Aspects of Musical Meter.* Oxford, UK: Oxford University Press.

THE SECRET OF THE DETAILS

Why is a groovy, swinging, or laid-back rhythm, despite all the timing differences, perceived as the same rhythm?

The rhythms that I have been talking about so far could all be notated as a series of ticks and rests. But just as with every musical notation, a representation such as this is, of course, a reduction of the music itself. A rhythm being played (or heard) can have all sorts of nuances that cannot be captured in such a notation. Differences can occur in the dynamics (a note may be played louder or softer); in the duration (a note may be held for a longer or shorter time); and in the color of the tone (the rhythm may be played on different instruments).

The most important nuances in a rhythm are associated with the timing. A lot of music must have the proper timing. If this is missing, then a fundamental element of that music is lost, and it becomes unpleasant to listen to. This is why, for many people, there is something magical about *timing*. And the magic, as so often is the case, rests in the details.

A rhythm can be played and heard in many ways: mechanically, swinging, laid-back, sped up, tight, groovy, expressive, jerky, etc. These are all terms used by musicians and listeners to indicate the quality of a rhythm.

All these nuances in musical perception are, for a large part, caused by some notes being played slightly too early or too late; often only a few milliseconds. How does a listener do that? How does one know that the rhythm has been "sped up" or that it's "swinging"? Why is a rhythm with a note that's a bit longer not just *another* rhythm? And, as a listener, how does one differentiate between timing and rhythm?

DOI: 10.4324/9781003158301-14

Rhythms that you notate on a grid-line (as we have done so far), with a tick or a rest at each position, can also be represented by a series of whole numbers. For example: the rhythm | |. | | (four notes or ticks with a rest in the middle) can also be represented in terms of the three proportional intervals *between* the notes. In that case, the distance between the first and the second note is one position on the grid, between the second and third notes two positions on the grid, and between the third and fourth notes, one position on the grid. That gives a ratio of 1:2:1.

These kinds of notation are also called *relative* or proportional representations, because they indicate how the durational intervals between the notes relate one with the other. (For example, in the above notation, the second note is twice as long as the first one.)

However we name it—this notation, in itself, still doesn't say anything about the *tempo* (the speed at which it's played) or the *timing* (whether a particular note is played too early or too late). But then, tempo and timing are often absent in music notation. It is often left to the musician to interpret the score. The tempo and timing are sometimes indicated by single or two-word directives, such as: *vivace* (fast, lively), *adagio* (slow, stately), *ritardando* (slowing down), *tempo rubato* (with variable tempo), or simply "with swing." The performing musician has to make do with this; he has to rely on his own knowledge of music to make these global directives audible to his audience in a specific piece of music.

Figure 10.1 Two ways to notate the same rhythm: as ticks and rests on a grid-line, drawn to a duration ratio of 1:2:1 (top) and in Western musical notation (bottom).

Also, for a researcher who wants to find out *what* is actually being played and how a listener assesses it, a glance at the score is insufficient. Words are not enough. It applies here too that "measuring is knowing."

If you were to ask a drummer to play the rhythm in the above example, and if you then measure the distance between the notes in seconds, then you would get something that would look like the following series of measurements (i.e., durations): 0.23–0.58–0.29. This is what we call an absolute representation: "absolute" because, from this series of measurements, the rhythm that was performed can be reproduced exactly (for instance with a computer).

But if we compare the series of durations 0.23–0.58–0.29 with the original ratio, namely 1:2:1, then there are important differences. Even if a drummer wants to play exactly what is written, and even if he does that with great conviction, he will never be able to play 1:2:1 exactly. A musician must take timing into account, whether he likes it or not. Even if he is asked to play exactly in time with a metronome (literally: keeping exactly to the notation), something of his own timing and phrasing will still remain. And more than that: even if the rhythm sounds metronomically precise, then that doesn't mean that it has been played exactly as indicated in the notation. (More on this later.)

The secret of the details rests largely on how a musician deals with these timing requirements. And it is these performance nuances that make the difference between one performance and another.

And from the listener's perspective? Is there anything to say about these performance nuances from that viewpoint?

WHICH RHYTHM DO WE HEAR?

A rhythm is actually performed along a continuous timeline; that is to say, not along a discrete grid-line as we have used for simplicity until now. Any position on this timeline can be expressed as a real number. We can now ask ourselves: When will the rhythm be heard as rhythm A, and when as rhythm B, because, for instance, it is played with some "swing?" As a listener, how does one differentiate between rhythm and timing?

To be able to answer these questions we need to look at "categorization"; the cognitive process by which people (and, as it turns out, most other animals as well) classify or divide objects in the world around them.

Figure 10.2 is an illustration of a somewhat longer rhythm. The upper part is the rhythm as it is played by a percussionist, while the lower part is the notation of it as a student at a music academy would notate it in a dictation on rhythm. For most of those music students, this would be a rather easy exercise. The upward arrow points at how the percussionist would perform the notated rhythm. The downward arrow points at the students notating that rhythm.

How do students at a music academy, and listeners in general, distil a series of *discrete* (countable) categories of notes (in other words, the whole numbers, or *integers*, shown above) from a series of continuous intervals while listening (in other words, the real numbers in the illustration above)? Interestingly a listener perceives, or better, classifies only a restricted, discrete number of note lengths while listening to such a performed rhythm. One can

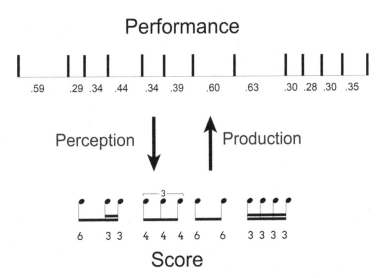

Figure 10.2 A rhythm as performed (top), and how it is consequently perceived and notated (bottom). The time intervals in italics are discussed in the text.

compare it with colours, which in our visual perception "clot" around blue, green, and red, while the color spectrum consists of a gradual continuously consecutive scale of colour wavelengths.

The downward pointing arrow in the image above illustrates the perceptual process known in cognitive sciences as "categorization," and in music software often referred to with the technical term *quantization*. The continuous timing of a performed rhythm can be separated into a symbolic, discrete rhythm and continuous timing by "quantizing."

Those who have worked with music notation software know, from experience, that it is quite a challenge to obtain a notation that resembles what you thought you just played on a keyboard. If not, try it out for yourself! You will find that the rhythm shown above, when performed on a drum pad or keyboard, will be notated in many small note lengths, for instance a demisemiquaver or a hemidemisemiquaver, as though it is a modernistic and rhythmically complex score.

As it turns out, the downward pointing arrow in Figure 10.2 (which represents the act of listening; the perception) cannot be explained as a simple rounding off process, in the way that 0.59 and 0.29 can be rounded off to the multiples of 0.10, 0.60, and 0.30. That can be clearly seen if, for example, one looks at the notes that are marked in the played rhythm (see the upper part of the illustration). There, the fifth interval is played *shorter* than the last interval (0.34 seconds instead of 0.35). If you now look at the notated rhythm (the lowest part of the illustration), then you will see that there, it is exactly the other way round: the fifth interval is heard as being *longer* than the last interval (4 is longer than 3).

So a computer program that simplistically rounds data off can never model or explain what a listener hears. It is evident that the context within which a rhythm is played greatly influences how a certain rhythm is categorized. But how exactly does that come about? And, what is even more important: how do you investigate that, systematically?

SUMMARY

We hear all kinds of details in rhythms that cannot be captured in a notation, such as variations in dynamics, duration, and timbre. The most important of such nuances are associated with *timing*. The secret of these details rests largely on how the musicians deal with the meaningful nuances of tempo and timing. Those who have worked with music notation software know, from experience, that it is quite a challenge to obtain a score that resembles what you thought you just played on a keyboard. Why is a mechanical or swinging version of a rhythm perceived as the same rhythm (while the timing differs)? And how much timing difference must there be before it becomes a different rhythm? This will be revealed in the next chapter.

FURTHER READING

Honing, H. & Bouwer, F. L. (2019). "Rhythm." In P. J. Rentfrow & D. Levitin (Eds.), *Foundations in Music Psychology: Theory and Research* (pp. 33–70). Cambridge, MA: The MIT Press.

PART 5
AHA! MUSIC IN OUR MINDS

THE SECRET, MAPPED OUT

How does one study rhythmic categorization? Is it possible to study all possible rhythms? What will a "rhythm space" (of all possible rhythms in all possible interpretations) look like?

Categorization was one of the topics in an ambitious research project that I carried out with the help of several colleagues at the beginning of this century. For this, we deliberately *didn't* look for as many music samples from different genres and music cultures as possible. The disadvantage of an approach such as that is that you never know for sure whether, somewhere, an exception will come to light that will destabilize the structural similarities that you have discovered. For that reason, we chose to design a method that allowed us to apply our analyses to all possible rhythms in *all* possible interpretations.

In the first place, we restricted ourselves to four-note rhythms, with three durations between them. We visualized this collection in a three-dimensional "rhythm space" in which every axis represents the length of one time interval (see Figure 11.1). Every point in that space represents a rhythm of three intervals of a certain length. This length is shorter if the point is close to the origin and longer if it is moved further away from the origin.

To reduce this (enormous) collection of rhythms somewhat, we only used rhythms of one second in total duration. That is a triangular cross-section of the same rhythm space (indicated in grey in Figure 11.1). All the illustrations in the rest of this chapter are positioned on this cross-section, which one can visualize as a triangle (see Figure 11.2). We call this a *chronotopological* chart ("chronos" = time, "topos" = place).

DOI: 10.4324/9781003158301-16

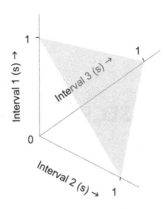

Figure 11.1 Rhythm space. A cross-section (in the shape of a triangle) indicates all rhythms of equal length, in this case, all rhythms with a length of one second.

That sounds more complicated than it is. In fact, it means nothing more than that each point in this flat triangle represents a four-note rhythm, the total duration of which is one second. That seems to be a magical reduction from three to two dimensions, but, in fact, it is very simple.

To give an example: rhythm A in Figure 11.2 has notes at the start, a quarter of a second, three-quarters of a second, and a whole second on the time axis. You can represent that with intervals as 0.25–0.50–0.25 sec. That rhythm is simply a single point in the triangle. To locate it, first find the value of the first interval on the relevant axis, and follow the line to the inside of the triangle, in the direction parallel with the side of the triangle. Then do the same for the other two intervals, and the point where the three arrows converge indicates the position of rhythm A (I will use the same visualization in the remainder of this chapter, so it is worth the trouble to learn how to navigate in the rhythm chart).

The rhythm space contains not only frequently occurring rhythms, but also very unusual ones. Within these, are sets of identical rhythms that have been timed in very different ways, such as "jerky" or "swinging." These are ways of performing that are never, seldom, or often used. So, what always turns out to be problematic in a set of specific samples is of no influence here, because there are no exceptions; all possible rhythmic proportions are included.

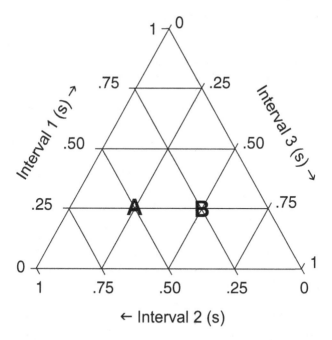

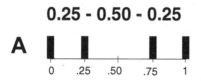

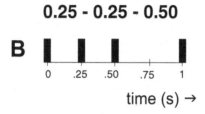

Figure 11.2 A chronotopological chart (top) and two sample rhythms (bottom).

WHAT ARE THE EXPECTATIONS?

A rhythm chart is very helpful in searching for an answer to the question of how listeners differentiate between rhythm and timing.

Suppose you give all like-sounding rhythms in the chart the same color or shade of grey. Will all versions or interpretations of a rhythm cluster around the "deadpan" (metronomical) version?

The illustration below shows two hypothetical rhythm charts that are only partly filled in (NB: this is not yet based on empirical facts, but on our fantasy). On the upper chart, the places indicated with an "x" represent metronomical rhythms (for example, 2:1:1). The grey areas around these represent the set of rhythms that have the same rhythm in the listeners' ears, even though, as far as timing goes, they sound a little bit different.

It is only a small step from this point to a completely empirical "listening chart": a chart that visualizes the results for all rhythms as perceived. How many islets can be seen? And what shape are they: round, square, or irregular? Are they all the same size? Do they all differ? Does each rhythm occur only once, or are there several islets for the same rhythm?

Other questions arise too. Are the islets situated close to each other and do they have distinct boundaries—a boundary that indicates the transition from one rhythmical category to another? Or do these areas overlap, so that there are no sharp boundaries between the categories? And if there are even smaller islets within those islets, do these represent families of rhythms in which a particular timing style predominates, such as all the rhythms that sound "mechanical" or "swinging" (see the lower chart, Figure 11.3)?

These are all questions that you can only formulate once you have "mapped" whole families of rhythms, rather than specific examples. Once done, it is then possible to formulate general hypotheses, which you can test by carrying out listening experiments. And only after that, will we arrive at the question: What do listeners actually hear?

First, consider how a commercial music notation program would notate various performed rhythms. In Figure 11.4, the lines mark the boundaries for rhythms that have been notated by the music notation program in the same way. The thick lines indicate the boundaries between these rhythmical categories. Two rhythms

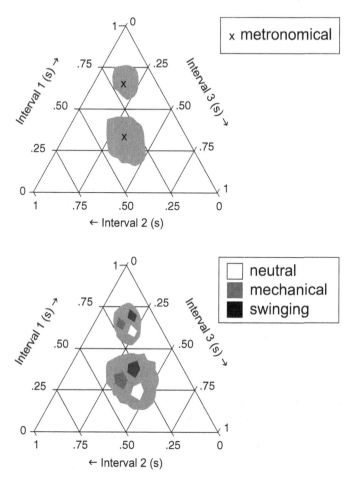

Figure 11.3 Hypothetical rhythm charts (top); islets around the metronomical rhythm (bottom); regions that indicate different timing qualities within a particular category.

within the same "islet" created by these boundaries are classified as being the same, two rhythms to either side of the boundary as differing from each other. Most of the islets turn out to be diamond shaped, and they are roughly of the same size.

In one of the first experiments of our research, we presented participants with a set of rhythms that were chosen in such a way

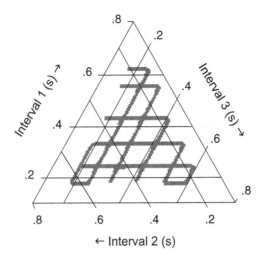

Figure 11.4 The category boundaries as predicted by a commercial music notation program.

that one could gain a good impression of the entire rhythm space. We then asked them to notate a large number of rhythms from this space. That's to say, we asked the participants to listen to each rhythm as though it was played by a drummer, and to notate what they thought would have been written in the drummer's score. In other words, the participants were asked to notate the category of the rhythm (equivalent to ratios such as: 1:3:1 or 1:2:1), measured in seconds (e.g., 0.23–0.48–0.29), that they had heard.

The results of that experiment are given in Figure 11.5. The thick lines again demarcate the boundaries between the different rhythm categories.

When comparing the above with the rhythm chart made by the notation program, what one notices immediately is that there are larger and smaller categories, and that they don't form anything like diamond shapes. Some rhythms can obviously be played with relatively widely differing timing without the listeners gaining the impression that they had heard another rhythm (e.g., 1:2:1 and 2:1:1). Other rhythms allowed hardly any variation in the timing (e.g., 2:3:1 and 3:1:4). If one slows down these rhythms, even marginally, then they will quickly be perceived as another rhythm.

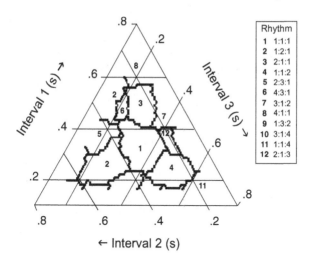

Figure 11.5 Empirically determined categories between various four-note rhythms.

The listeners didn't always give the same response. Each depicted islet is, in fact, a mountain, the summit of which indicates the rhythm notated by the majority of listeners—the "modal" or most frequently occurring rhythm. In almost all cases, it became evident that this modal rhythm was not the exact metronomic version, but a rhythm with a bit of timing. And that's surprising!

The majority of listeners wrote down 1:1:1 for a rhythm that was timed as 0.33–0.31–0.36 seconds, which was the most frequently selected notation for that rhythm; a minority of listeners notated 1:1:1 for the rhythm 0.33–0.33–0.33, which is the (metronomic) rhythm as indicated by the score.

If the last-mentioned rhythm is "phrased" a little (e.g., slowed down at the end, with a small ritardando) then, apparently, that rhythm will sound more like the notated rhythm than if a computer had played the rhythm exactly as notated. So, if you want a performance to sound as though it is being played exactly in accordance with the way it is notated in the score, then the rhythm should not be played metronomically (musicians use the word "tightly"), but with a slight deceleration—with a *ritardando*. [1]

This research also taught us that timing cannot just be defined as a deviation from what is notated in the score. A more realistic interpretation is that it is the most frequently heard performance of a rhythm—rather than the notation of it—that starts to function as the reference. So it is best to define timing as a deviation from the most frequently heard version of a rhythm.

CAN YOU HEAR IT DIFFERENTLY?

How sharp are the boundaries between the different categories of rhythm that we hear? Is there any evidence of a gradual transition from one category to another, or is the transition relatively abrupt?

Imperviousness to nuances, this last-mentioned research question, is known as "categorical perception," and is defined as the automatic classification of a certain sensory phenomenon in a clearly defined, known category.

There is, however, rather a lot of discussion about the question of when a rhythmic phenomenon should be viewed as a categorical perception. It seems clear to me that a definition that leads to the conclusion that listeners are insensitive to differences in nuances in timing is untenable, because that's exactly what many people value so much in music; obviously, rhythm perception cannot easily be separated from other sorts of contextual information. On the other hand, as we saw in the rhythm chart in Figure 11.6, listeners subconsciously attribute rhythms they hear performed to reputable categories. However, a rhythm that is played identically, and is physically the same, can sound totally different in another context, and so is perceived and experienced in another way.

To examine this last-mentioned phenomenon, we asked a group of listeners to take part in a listening experiment featuring the same rhythms as in the previous experiment, but in which the same rhythms were now preceded by a rhythmical fragment in either 2/4 or 3/4 time. The resulting rhythm chart changed enormously. This supplied the evidence we had predicted to find, and we could now say with confidence that the context in which a rhythm is played greatly influences the way in which that rhythm is heard.

To substantiate the evidence described above, I would like to close this chapter by going into even more detail about the outcomes of these last-mentioned experiments.

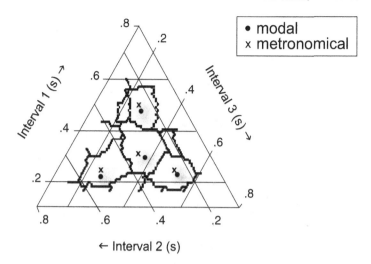

Figure 11.6 An empirical rhythm chart showing the position of the metronomic and modal (most frequently notated) rhythm for each of the biggest categories.

In the first experiment, the participants were asked to listen to rhythms that were preceded by rhythmic fragments in duple meter (see the upper rhythm chart in Figure 11.7 on the next page). The result was that, compared with the previous experiment without a preceding rhythm, some areas of the rhythm chart became larger and other areas, smaller. (Compare, for example, the central islets for the rhythm 1:1:1 in Figure 11.7 on the next page with those in Figure 11.6 above)

In the second experiment, the participants were presented rhythms that were preceded by a fragment played in triple meter (see the lower rhythm chart in Figure 11.7). The results: some rhythmic categories disappeared, and new ones appeared on the rhythm chart (for example, the rhythmic category 1:3:2 in the earlier charts disappeared, but it became a large area 9 in the lower rhythm chart in Figure 11.7).

Conclusion: the way in which a physically identical rhythm is categorized depends on what someone has heard earlier. In this way, the rhythm 0.26–0.42–0.32, preceded by a fragment of music played in 2/4 time, was heard by most of the participants as 1:2:1.

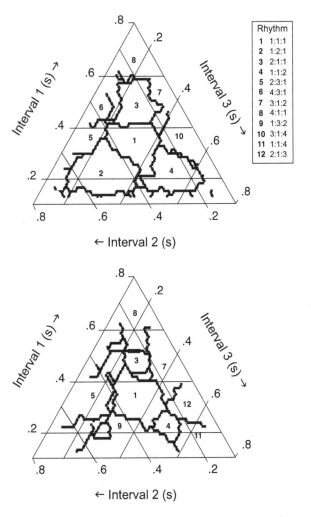

Figure 11.7 Category boundaries between different rhythms heard, preceded
by a rhythm in duple meter (top) and in triple meter (bottom).

However, when the same rhythm was preceded by a fragment of
music in 3/4 time, then most participants heard that as 1:3:2.

What happened in these two (sub)experiments, was replicated in
all our listening experiments. Time and again, the metrical

structure of the fragment that preceded a rhythm appeared to determine the category in which it would be placed by the participants in the experiment. We also discovered all sorts of patterns in the different rhythm charts, such as that a rhythm only ever appears in one islet on the rhythm chart. This is a useful discovery, because a pattern such as this makes it a lot easier to develop "comprehensive" computational models of rhythm perception.

DOES THIS DISCLOSE THE SECRET?

The systematic study of rhythm and timing reveals how tricky it is—though not impossible—to identify and chart nuances in music scientifically. Moreover, the research described above also has its limitations. One of these is related to the so-called "identification task" we used: the participants were asked to note down carefully what they had heard. This is a task that assumes specialized skills; not everyone has these skills. For that reason, the group of potential participants was restricted to those with knowledge of Western music notation, such as professional musicians and students at music academies. Ordinary listeners, or those that are familiar with or grew up in other (music) cultures, were not invited to take part.

Recently, however, music psychologist Nori Jacoby of the Max Planck Institute of Empirical Aesthetics in Germany devised an alternative method that is not dependent on music notation: a method where participants basically just have to tap along with a selected rhythm from the rhythm space. The authors could show that the rhythm space obtained in this way shows "islets" that closely overlap with those obtained with the identification task discussed above. Interestingly, the resulting rhythmic categories were found to be similar for Westerners, *irrespective* of their musical expertise. As such, the study replicated the results discussed above, but, even more important, shows that there are only subtle differences between (Western) ordinary and expert listeners.

An ambitious next step in this research was to do the same experiment in a variety of cultures. The first results included a rhythm chart of listeners from an Amazonian hunter/gatherer society (the Tsimané). And here as well, the resulting rhythm chart featured peaks at similar integer ratios as Western listeners.

But there were also important cross-cultural differences. For example, whereas native Amazonians share some rhythmic categories (integer ratio rhythms), the study also revealed distinct categories (such as 2:3:2) that are not observed in Western listeners.

Overall, the results can be characterized as a combination of favouring time intervals that are related by simple integer ratios, combined with an asymmetric distribution (see Figure 11.6 on p. 121) that might reflect the impact of exposure to timing patterns typical to a certain culture.

In summary: the ability to hear nuances in the timing of a piece of music is the outcome of the cognitive process of categorization, which, in turn, is determined by our memory, our expectations, and the ways in which we have been exposed to music in the course of our lives. A listener does not hear rhythm and timing as an abstract unity, as is notated in music scores, nor as a continuum in the way that physicists describe time. "No": he, she, and we hear rhythm, timing, and music in what one might call "clots": the denser areas that can be seen on the rhythm charts. While listening, the time *clumps* around the rhythms that we often, and with a certain timing, have heard. Our listening experience reinforces itself. The more we have listened, the more we differentiate.

That is why, after this long, educative pause, we should quickly return to the concert hall. The *maestro* and the orchestra are ready to treat us to new and old, familiar, and surprising music.

SUMMARY

A *chronotopological* chart, that maps out our rhythm perception, can be very helpful in searching for an answer to the question of how listeners differentiate between rhythm and timing. The idea that listeners are insensitive to differences in nuances in timing is untenable, because it's exactly these nuances many people appreciate in music. Listeners subconsciously attribute rhythms they hear performed to reputable categories.

NOTE

1 The same effect can be found in other domains where categorization is researched—such as in facial research. There as well, an exaggeration of the facial features often gives a more recognizable impression than the original.

FURTHER READING

Jacoby, N. & McDermott, J. H. (2017). "Integer ratio priors on musical rhythm revealed cross-culturally by iterated reproduction." *Current Biology*, 27, 359–370.

THE MUSICAL LISTENER

Is everybody musical? What do we know about the musical skills of the ordinary listener?

Of course, my claim that everyone is intrinsically musical should be taken "with a grain of salt." It gives the impression that musicality should come naturally to every one of us. Nevertheless, in the previous pages, I hope that I have convinced the reader that there is real substance in the thesis that everyone is musical. This applies not only to inborn elements, or to ones that develop spontaneously, but also to skills that, given favourable circumstances, can blossom with diligent study, copious practice, and a steadfast belief in one's own capacity. Musicality sometimes amounts to unlearning, in the sense that we shed certain sensitivities influenced by the musical culture in which we have grown up.

In this chapter, using a number of prominent studies undertaken in recent years, I will demonstrate that all this is reality rather than theory. Three listening experiments will be reviewed: the first using adults, children, and babies; the second using trained musicians; and the third group using what I will call "ordinary" everyday listeners. This diversity helps us to gain a good insight into the differences and similarities between these groups of listeners.

In earlier studies, the listening skills of musicians and non-musicians were contrasted, one with the other, to some extent. However, recent studies show that if all the participants are familiar with the music used in the experiments, providing the tasks can be carried out by all the participants, irrespective of whether or not they know the names of notes, or how the black and white keys on the piano are organized, then often, the differences between these two groups are

DOI: 10.4324/9781003158301-17

not so very large. And where there are differences, then they will be relatively small; certainly, if we set these against the thousands of hours that most musicians have invested in their specialization.

A LECTURE FOR CHILDREN

"Which of you is musical?" I asked a group of children during a talk I gave at the science museum in Amsterdam not too long ago. The reaction of the fifty or so listeners, aged between eight and twelve years, was not very different from that of a room full of adults: about a quarter hesitantly raised a finger.

I always take children seriously, but when I questioned them a bit further, it turned out that they interpreted the question as: Can you play the piano or violin well? or even, Do your parents think you can play the piano well?

Spontaneously, members of my young audience started to tell all sorts of stories about their own, or someone else's, lack of musicality: a father who has no sense of rhythm and cannot dance; a sister who always sings out of tune—terrible! I also hear stories at the other end of the spectrum, such as a friend with a fantastic sense of rhythm, whose drumming is "out of this world."

During the talk, I tried to explain why one can also be musical, even if one doesn't play an instrument. My message obviously got through: at the end of the talk, interspersed by short listening tests, my young audience had become much more positive. In answer to the question "Which of you is musical?" almost everyone put their hands up. That's something to make a scientist happy!

A SENSE OF RHYTHM

I had borrowed one of the listening tests that I presented during my talk, from an ingeniously devised study set up by developmental scientists Erin E. Hannon and Sandra E. Trehub in 2005. Their aim was to find out to what extent one's sense of rhythm is influenced by the musical culture in which people grow up. To that end, they let about fifty North American adults listen to Serbian and Bulgarian folksongs. Half of these songs were composed in a simple meter such as a march (duple meter) or a waltz (triple meter), both of them well-known meters for enthusiasts of Western music. The other half was composed in a more complex meter such as the 5/8 and 7/8 time often used in Bulgarian and Macedonian music.

After that, the participants were asked to listen to each folksong again, in two variants. In the first variant, a note was added to the drum rhythm without changing the structure of the meter. In other words, the note was made "congruent" with the meter by, for example, replacing one note with two short notes adding up to the same duration. In the second variant, a note was added repeatedly, but without changing the lengths of the notes on either side, so that the drum rhythm gained an extra count, which then conflicted with the meter. In other words, it was "incongruent" with the meter.

The question posed was: Which variant is the same or rhythmically congruent, and which isn't?

In the folksongs with simple meters, it turned out that all the participants were able to differentiate between the congruent and the incongruent variants. But in the folksongs with a more complex meter, half of the participants pointed to one variant and the other half to the other. Expressed differently, their scores were similar to those of people who were just guessing.

It will probably be the same for the majority of readers if they were to try doing this test. The differences in the rhythm are more noticeable in a folksong with a simple meter than in one where the meter is complex. Why is that? Are we only able to manage simple songs?

One of the surprises of this research came to light when the researchers asked volunteers with Bulgarian or Macedonian backgrounds to listen to the same folksongs. It turned out that they were able to hear the rhythmical differences in the complex meter variants just as well as in the simple meter variants. Obviously, the music culture in which they were raised had influenced their sense of rhythm. In other words, by simply being exposed to certain types of music—in the case of the Macedonians, music in which complex meters often occur—the listener unconsciously picks up the statistical regularity of the rhythms used in the music.

A second surprise came to light in the last group of listeners that Hannon and Trehub researched: six-month-old babies from North America. Just as for the Bulgarian adults, it transpired that these babies were sensitive to the rhythmical differences in both types of meter. For this experiment, the "head-turning paradigm," mentioned earlier, that measures the time that a baby maintains an interest in something, proved very useful. If a baby heard something new, then it looked longer in the direction of the loudspeaker. If the baby found it boring, then the "looking time" was shorter.

At first, this last observation seemed to contradict the idea that sense of rhythm is influenced by culture, because there was no indication of this in these North American babies. However, if one combines the results of all three listening experiments, then one can but conclude that the exception is not these babies, but the adult North American listeners. Almost everyone is born with the skill to differentiate between different meters, but the older the person, the more their sense of rhythm deteriorates if they are not exposed to certain complex rhythms. Therefore, the musical culture with which one grows up is more likely to determine what remains of the sense of rhythm, than what is added.

That idea was substantiated in a later study, in which one-year-old babies participated. At that age, the differences between babies and adults have become smaller. Within half a year, the sensitivity of babies to differences in rhythm equates more with that of adult listeners.

To gain a more exact picture of which attributes are inborn and which are acquired or are culture-specific, the researchers also examined the possible effects of exposure. Could listening to unfamiliar music for two weeks prior to the experiment have any influence on the results?

Two groups, one of adults and the other of parents with babies between eleven and twelve months old, were given a CD of dance music from Macedonia, Bulgaria, and Bosnia to take home with them, performed in the combined meters characteristic of those countries. They were asked to play the CD twice a day. Neither group had ever heard that sort of music before.

The outcome was that this hardly had any effect on the group of adults. Their total score was almost the same as that of the other group of North American listeners who had not listened to the CD. As an adult, how long does one need to listen to unfamiliar rhythms before being able to notice the difference between rhythms that are comparable? If one takes this research literally: at least twice a day for more than two weeks.

The twelve-month-old babies appeared to be much more flexible. After they had been regularly confronted with Balkan music for two weeks, they were much more sensitive to differences than babies of the same age who had not listened to the CD. Even though, after a year, babies' sensitivity to unfamiliar rhythms deteriorates significantly, their brains are extremely flexible and resilient. Also, after their first year, they are receptive to new, unfamiliar music.

Adults' brains are much less flexible, so it is more difficult for them to recognize rhythmical patterns from an unfamiliar musical culture (or to learn a second language). They have adapted themselves, as it were, to the musical structure of their own culture. It doesn't seem too implausible, then, that frequent and varied listening at a young age helps to develop the listening skills from which we derive much pleasure as adults.

But is the opposite also true? As an adult, is it pointless listening to new and unfamiliar music?—of course not! Whoever, as a Westerner, raised with Western music, wants to deepen their knowledge of, for example, Chinese opera, can be largely successful in achieving that aim, but they will have to put much more effort into it than either a baby, or an adult who has been raised within the Chinese musical culture and tradition.

In addition, there are many aspects of music, other than sense of rhythm that are not linked to a short critical period, such as sense of timing, harmony, and new musical styles. I will deal with these aspects one by one below.

TIMING

Frequent listeners to classical radio stations (at least this is the case in the Netherlands) are undoubtedly familiar with the programs in which a number of experts are asked to listen to recordings of two or more fragments of classical music. They are asked to guess the name of the composition and which musicians are playing, and to give their opinion of the performances and say which one they prefer. For experienced professional musicians, one would think they would be able to do this confidently; more so than ordinary listeners. And, indeed, stacked-up superlatives and contemptuous disapproval fly through the air at those points in these programs.

To establish whether experts *really* hear more than ordinary listeners, in 2006, together with a number of musicology students from the University of Amsterdam and Olivia Ladinig, who has meanwhile gained her doctorate, I set up a research project on listening. We wanted to establish how, in fact, experts are able to evaluate nuances in the timing of different performances, and the extent to which this is dependent upon their expertise. The underlying question was this: Do people develop their capacity to differentiate by *listening* to music very often, or by *knowing* a lot about it? In other words, is this all about exposure or expertise?

From one of our first experiments (on the Internet) the outcome was that, indeed, experts were very good at recognizing differences in timing. We let them hear two versions of the same piano composition: the "actual" performance, and one in which we had changed the tempo. For this, we used recordings of famous pianists, among them Glenn Gould and Sviatoslav Richter, both of whom had performed the same movement of Bach's English Suites. As one would expect, Gould performed it much faster than Richter, by about 20 percent.

In addition, we changed the tempo of both recordings electronically, to create two new pairs: one in which Gould's recording was slowed down to match that of Richter, and another one in which Richter's recording was sped up to match that of Gould. In each case, the pitch and other characteristics of the sound were retained.

The participants in the experiment were challenged with the task to identify which of the two recordings was the actual performance. Even had one been able to identify the recording (we used quite a few famous ones), it would have been impossible to derive this from the tempo, because that was now the same for both sound fragments in the pair that had to be compared. In addition, for Glenn Gould, we had chosen movements from his *Goldberg Variations*, played in tempos that varied greatly, one from the other.[1]

By changing the tempo of the recording, the phrasing and the timing of a performance sounded strange or unnatural: the music "breathes" differently. (Compare this with old black and white films that are projected fractionally faster than they were made. When projected, the image on those kinds of film is always unnatural and sped up.) If a musician plays a piece faster or slower, then he adapts his timing to the new tempo, because expressive timing is tempo specific. The prevailing idea is that experts are better able to judge whether these variations sound "natural" or "strange" than amateurs. And, indeed, about 70 percent of the participants in our test could hear which of the two performances had been manipulated.

So, as yet, there was nothing surprising to report. The majority of the participants were familiar with the piano works of Bach, Beethoven, Schumann, and Chopin, and they had accumulated years of experience as amateur or professional musicians, mostly as pianists. But now we knew for sure that experienced musicians can hear from the timing whether a performance has been recorded in another tempo. This provided us with good comparative material for our next listening experiment on the Internet, which was aimed at comparing the "achievements" of music experts with those of ordinary listeners.

In this new experiment, we used different sorts of music and invited listeners with a very wide range of musical backgrounds and preferences to take part in it. We received hundreds of reactions to the various invitations that we placed in the media and on Internet forums; enough to make a selection based on musical education and preference and to create a representative group for each genre of music.

Again, we asked the participants to compare, at home and from their own computer, a series of performance pairs. This time, however, they were in three different genres: rock, classical, and jazz. The participants listened to a total of sixty fragments, in half of which the tempo had been changed.

The classical fragments were the same as for the earlier experiment with musically educated listeners. For the jazz section, we asked participants to listen to recordings of Miles Davis and Bill Evans, while the rock fans were treated to Iggy Pop and Jimi Hendrix.

The first surprise was that the experts' score was not significantly better than that of the ordinary listeners. A classical music enthusiast without specific education in music could hear the differences in timing just as well as a professional pianist who had studied music for many years. Also, on average, a professional rock musician could do this just as well as someone who listened to rock purely for pleasure. In other words, explicit knowledge of music does not automatically mean that the person will be more sensitive to the timing nuances in music. Implicit knowledge, gathered by listening frequently to music, appears to be just as effective—a surprising result!

A second surprise was that familiarity with the repertoire (whether rock, jazz, or classical) greatly influenced the participants' answers: they scored better with fragments from their preferred genre. Although so-called lay people may be unable to give a *technical explanation* of why one particular number performed by Jimi Hendrix sounded better than another, they hear the differences nevertheless.

The research on babies showed that the brain becomes less receptive to rhythms that are not listened to. The same applies to adults—but then in reverse. By listening a lot to a certain type of music, one hears the nuances better, even better than professionals who are specialized in another genre. A classically trained musician hears in the *horrible noise* of amplified recordings played by the teenagers next door by far not as many, nor the same, nuances that make this horrible noise so attractive to teenagers.

From these combined results, we could conclude that a person's musicality—in our case focused on timing—is mainly influenced by the music they listen to most. Expertise or a musical education has no measurable influence on this type of listening skill.

HARMONY

Most of the examples in this book relate to aspects of time in music: rhythm, meter, timing, but similar results have been found in the areas of melody and harmony.

All of us have relative pitch: even if the greengrocer whistles one of Frank Sinatra's tunes lower or slower, we can immediately recognize which song it is (see Chapter 8). Without realizing it, we often recognize the underlying harmonic structure of a piece of music, and we then use that knowledge while listening to it. A melody can be arranged by a jazz trio, for example, to incorporate tunes such as Waterloo, Walking on the Moon, or Isobel into their repertoire. In such cases the melody is not retained exactly, but, nevertheless, after a few bars, we can already hear that it is an arrangement of a well-known tune.

No matter how different the melody and rhythm are in a performance, we can recognize the underlying pattern of chords and from that the tune itself. Although the "surface structure" of the music may be very different, the deeper underlying harmonic structure is recognizably the same, and the chord pattern stays the same. Almost everyone, mostly without realizing it, is sensitive to the underlying structure, the harmony. We interpret a fragment of music as a variation of a known tune, and that evokes the expectation that the music will continue in a certain way. If we didn't have the harmonic expectation, for example because we don't know or recognize the tune, then the jazz improvisation would rapidly sound chaotic. In fact, it is the (pro)active "listening along," the nurturing of strong melodic and harmonic expectations that are confirmed on one occasion and disfigured the next that, for some people, is the "jazz" of the jazz.

It is possible, also in harmony, to gauge the listener's expectation with precision. An excellent example is the experiment that Emmanuel Bigand and Barbara Tillmann carried out with trained musicians and non-musicians—lay people. For this, they had a number of melodies composed that differed very much, one from the other, with respect to melodic contour and rhythm, but, as a collection, had the same underlying pattern of chords. The melodies from a certain collection could, as it were, be accompanied by the same chords, without them sounding strange. What differed was that the chords were not actually audible; they were, as it were, implied by the melody, in the same way as a meter can be implied or induced by a rhythm.

The assignment put to the two groups—the experts and the lay people—was to identify which of the melodic variations had the same underlying harmonic structure, or, in other words, which belonged to the same collection. In this experiment, the trained musicians did better than the non-musicians, but what was interesting was that the non-musicians did much better than one would have expected on the basis of chance. It seems that ordinary listeners are also able to recognize harmonic structure and from this are able to link up different melodies.

The majority of listening experiments carried out by Bigand's research group, used relatively simple melodies played in a quasi-classical style. However, it wouldn't surprise me if it were found that the differences between trained musicians and non-musicians became even smaller if the same experiment was carried out using music to which we are all regularly exposed, such as pop music.

In any case, what the experiment described above (and the various related studies) shows is that all listeners absorb musical information abstractly into their "system"—they internalize it. We remember melodies in a relative way, rather than exactly. Apart from the intervals and the changes in pitch, we also remember the tonal relationship between the notes.

While listening, we use the retained, internalized, knowledge about harmony to enable us to interpret a melody harmonically. Our expectations in this respect can be so forthright that a relatively large change in a melody goes unnoticed, because it fits into the tonal frameworks to which we are accustomed. If you were to get young babies to listen to the same fragment, then they would certainly notice a change like this; an indication that, in them, these harmonic expectations have not yet developed.

Assuming that a person's musical knowledge is strongly influenced by the regularities of the musical culture in which they have been raised and/or born, shouldn't we expect listeners who, as a group of individuals, have grown up in *different* musical cultures to have diverse harmonic expectations? It's an intriguing question!

Unfortunately, very little comparative research has been carried out on this aspect, but the little that has, points in the direction of a "yes."

In a somewhat older study, the music psychologist Carol Krumhansl and associates compare and contrast the musical experiences of listeners with North American, North Indian, and Balinese backgrounds. For this, they used the frequently applied probe-tone test in which the volunteer is asked to listen to a melody followed by a constantly changing closing note. This final note has to be evaluated: How strongly does the person expect to hear that note from the melody? Or, to put it in another way, does the note sound like a closing note to that melody, or does it raise other expectations?

This study showed that the Balinese volunteers had indeed expected to hear other closing notes than the Western participants in the experiment. Moreover, it became clear that, to adapt to the expectation patterns of music from another culture, some habituation is enough. All the listeners were subconsciously sensitive to the patterns of the music from their own musical culture, whether Balinese, North Indian, or Western. However, they were also responsive to the idiosyncrasies of unfamiliar kinds of music, providing they were confronted with it often enough.

STYLE

If you sit in your car and turn the knob of the radio a little, you can hear immediately whether certain music is to your liking or not. You recognize a voice, a tune, or even by whom it's performed. Everyone does it; everyone can do it, and often extremely quickly, quicker than the sound of the average note.

If you were to be asked to listen to a series of musical fragments, each lasting 0.2 seconds, you would find that you had no trouble in identifying from which musical genre the fragment came: classical, jazz, R&B, or pop. A snippet of sound helps us to recall music that we have heard at an earlier date, even though we may never have heard this particular series of notes before. The recollection can be very specific: one of Björk's tunes, for example. But it can also be rather general: we recognize a certain genre—classical, country, jazz. The timbres characteristic of a song or a whole genre are apparently stored abstractly in our memories. (That is why the dial—or touch control—of the car radio has become such a successful interface).

Of course, the longer the sound fragment, the more we recognize. Music researcher Simone Dalla Bella showed that listeners are easily able to differentiate between various musical styles and can indicate from which historical period compositions originate, and all that without having had one music lesson. For his experiment, Dalla Bella had short piano compositions made that imitated different musical styles, from baroque to romantic and post romantic. All the pieces composed in the same key and meter, were performed in more or less the same tempo, and lasted for about half a minute. Again, both trained musicians and non-musicians took part in the experiment and both groups were asked to indicate which of two performances might have been composed earlier.

By far the majority of the participants could place the performances in the correct historical order. Although, also here, the musicians scored just a bit better than the non-musicians, it was surprising that listeners who had never deliberately listened to classical music, completed the assignment just as well. Simply being exposed, and as such becoming acquainted with music, seemed to be the most obvious explanation for this.

SUMMARY

Listening experiences of adults, children, babies, as well as "ordinary" and professional listeners give interesting insights into differences and similarities between these groups. It turns out that all listeners (whether musically trained or not), simply by being exposed to certain types of music, unconsciously pick up the statistical regularities of the styles of music they listen to. A revealing study with six-month-old North American babies showed that they were sensitive to rhythmic variations in unfamiliar music, a skill that their parents lacked, but that are easily picked up by adult listeners with a Bulgarian or Macedonian background. This suggests that rhythm perception is a combination of nature and nurture. While we clearly have an innate predisposition to recognize rhythms (and their timing)—if you do not use it, you lose it. However, with enough exposure to unfamiliar music, as adults we are still able to learn all kinds of novel aspects like sense of timing, harmony, or appreciate new musical styles.

NOTE

1 To ensure that participants didn't simply select the manipulated performance because of artifacts in the sound that could have been caused by the computer program, we asked a group of sound experts to concentrate just on the quality of the sound, and, for each performance, to say whether or not they thought it had been manipulated. With a few exceptions, they were unable to do this.

FURTHER READING

Ashley, R. & Timmers, R. (2017). *The Routledge Companion to Music Cognition*. Abingdon, UK: Routledge.

Hallam, S., Cross, I., & Thaut, M. (2016). *The Oxford Handbook of Music Psychology*. Oxford, UK: Oxford University Press.

Rentfrow, P. J. & Levitin, D. J. (Eds.) (2019). *Foundations in Music Psychology: Theory and Research*. Cambridge, MA: The MIT Press.

LISTENING AND LEARNING

Would listening to atonal music make it as familiar and as popular as other music we like to listen to? Who contributes most to a thrilling listening experience: the composer, the musician or the listener?

All the research described in the previous chapters shows that responsiveness to melody and rhythm is supported by two pillars: inborn sensitivity and the capacity to learn. It also shows that by no means does learning have to take place within formal school-like frameworks. People can also gain knowledge and insight into the structure and regularities of melodies and rhythms by simply listening to music. This explains the clear contrasts between adult listeners from different cultures.

Are such differences also evident within a culture? Is it true, to use the composer Arnold Schönberg's wording of it, that atonal music, such as serial music or aleatoric music, would sound just as familiar as classical or popular music if people listened to it often enough? Or is atonal music, with its mathematical transformations, such as "inversion," "transposition," and "retrograde," so distanced from the "laws" of our cognitive system, that many of the structures used in the music cannot be perceived by our hearing?

When Schönberg's colleague Pierre Boulez was asked this question in 1999, he responded as follows: "Perhaps we [the atonal composers] didn't pay enough attention to the way in which listeners actually hear music." A striking reaction from someone who stood at the cradle of serial composing!

Is it appropriate for Boulez to confess "guilt" here? Is it really always necessary to adhere to the listener's pattern of expectations? Or should composers risk the punishment of not being "heard?"

DOI: 10.4324/9781003158301-18

No. Cognitively incomprehensible music can also be very attractive, perhaps just because of its incomprehensibility. It's like poetry, which is often exciting for much the same reason. As I said before, it can do no harm, once in a while, to "play" with our cognitive functions. It makes us aware of the chains by which the rules of the game, arising from our cognitive functions, restrain our listening, causing, in the case of compositions that are neither "normal" nor tonal, music to become almost intangible, like a piece of wet soap.

To return now to the question of whether we should be able to discern and appreciate the underlying principles of atonal, serial music, and the mathematical transpositions they contain, and if not, whether it is possible to learn how to recognize these principles. Was Schönberg correct in what he said?

Not many experiments have been carried out yet in this area, but the studies that *have* been undertaken, show that, in general, it's very difficult to identify the transpositions in serial music just by listening. Zoltán Dienes and Christopher Longuet-Higgins asked both musicians and non-musicians to listen to a number of melodies that, complying with the rules of serial music, were based on an orderly series of twelve notes. In a series like this, every note from a chromatic scale (a scale containing all the twelve notes in the Western tuning system) is used once. After that, the note cannot be repeated until all the other notes in the scale have been played once.

It's a hard-and-fast rule, which, together with a number of other ones, advocates a kind of democratization of music. Because each note in the melody is equally as important as the next, it must, therefore, be played just as frequently. This is the opposite of tonal music in which, to give an example, the tonic (the first note of a major or minor scale) occurs more frequently than the other notes, and therefore seems more "important."

The participants in Dienes and Longuet-Higgins' experiment were asked to listen to a series of short melodies, comprising two melodies of six notes at each stage. They were asked to say whether or not these melodies were related. The ones that were related were based on the same fragment of a twelve-note series, but they were sometimes presented as a transposition—a mirroring or reversal of the first six notes of the melody. The melodies that were not related had been arranged in another, non-serial way, for use in this experiment.

The outcome was that hardly any of the participants could distinguish related melodies from those which were not. Only a few professional musicians, who were familiar with modern performance practice, were able to do that, but only then for certain specific transpositions. Moreover, further questioning revealed that these same musicians had, in fact, cheated: they had used all sorts of memory aids and calculation rules to keep the original melody and the variations separate from each other in order to compare them. Once again, this confirms the overall conclusion of the research, that our ears are hardly able to hear some of the structures used by serial composers, and that we cannot learn how to overcome this problem.

So, was Schönberg wrong? No, because other researchers came to different conclusions. Emmanuel Bigand's group, mentioned earlier, had devised an experiment focused on the basic material of serial music—a complete series of twelve notes. (Dienes and Longuet-Higgins only used a half series—six notes.) In addition, they had worked with samples of substantial length. They arranged for 40 different *canons* to be composed in serial style, each of them about 20 seconds in time length. The volunteers were then asked to group the canons based on the same scale, and those based on other scales.

Most of the participants—62 percent of the musicians' group and 61 percent of the non-musicians' group—were able to complete this task well. Although these were not exceptionally high scores, they were high enough for the researchers to feel justified in assuming that concentrated listening also makes it possible to distinguish, to some extent, between unfamiliar musical structures. And again, it was also evident that musicians did not, by definition, score better than ordinary listeners.

BACKSTAGE, TO THE ARTISTS' GREENROOM

Does this mean that composers and musicians don't matter too much when it comes to the final listening experience? So from now on, should we consider the listener as the *prima donna* of music practice?

Of course, not! In the final chapter of this book I deliberately go backstage to the greenroom, where the composers and musicians are waiting. Now that listeners have had the chance—and grasped it—to demonstrate that music doesn't exist without them, the main priority now is to bring the composers and musicians back on stage, before the lights dim.

Music is an interplay: a game with the performing musician, the composer, and the listener in the main roles. It was modern composers in particular, who, thirty years ago, prompted me to listen to unfamiliar music and made me curious to know more. It was the musicians who, on more than one occasion during the past three decades, made me dizzy with a harmonic phrase or a deferred note that gave me, as a listener, an unforgettable musical experience. Fortunately, I'm no exception by far. The musician, the composer, and the listener: all three of them are essential to the quintessentially human activity that we call "music."

Encore!

SUMMARY

Our responsiveness to melody and rhythm is supported by an inborn sensitivity to musical structures and by our capacity to learn. Cognitively incomprehensible music can be very enjoyable just because of its incomprehensibility. Concentrated listening makes it possible to distinguish between unfamiliar musical structures; and, when tested, ordinary listeners score pretty much the same as professional musicians.

FURTHER READING

Ross, A. (2007). *The Rest is Noise: Listening to the Twentieth Century*. New York: Farrar, Strauss and Giroux.

ENCORE

How to teach a computer to conduct? Can computers improve our knowledge of music? What other methodologies contribute to our understanding of our capacity for music? What does the future of music cognition look like?

I will close with a personal afterword on what brought me to the field of music cognition, a story in which, initially, the computer played an important role, and where, much later, psychology and biology joined in. Imagine yourself in the audience, and enjoy what's going to happen on stage!

1988: A COMPOSITION FOR TWO PERCUSSIONISTS (AND A "CONDUCTING" COMPUTER)

Two percussionists with bright yellow sound-dampers over their ears are standing back-to-back on a fine, well-lit stage, as though a classical duel between two men fighting for their honour was about to begin. They step away from each other and begin to play, each with their own repetitive rhythm.

There are earphones underneath the sound-dampers. These enable the percussionists to hear themselves playing, but not their fellow musician. Both players are linked to a computer located at the center of the stage. All the musical information is fed continuously into the computer as zeros and ones through thick cables running across the floor. The computer "listens" and, in the first phase of the composition, imitates exactly the rhythm that the percussionists are tapping on a wood-block. The two percussionists hear themselves in their own ears via the "ears" of the computer.

DOI: 10.4324/9781003158301-19

The computer then begins to "conduct," but the audience is not aware of this because the computer is positioned motionless on the stage. However, via the earphones, it tries to influence the percussionists by making slight changes to the rhythm they are listening to and performing at the same time. Step-by-step, the computer suggests small changes in the rhythm, and checks continually to see whether its musicians have accepted and implemented its suggestions.

The first thing that the computer tries to do is to get the musicians to play in the same tempo. If one percussionist ignores its suggestion to play a bit faster, then, channelled back via the headphones, it tries to get the other percussionist to slow down by playing his reverberating rhythm a little bit slower. After a few minutes of these inaudible negotiations, the computer gets its own way. Now, both percussionists are playing at the same speed: end of the first movement. The percussionists take one step away from each other.

Duel has five movements in all (see Figure 14.1), each of them characterized by a dramatically threatening step moving the percussionists further away from each other. Beginning with a random repetitive rhythm, they end up playing exactly the same rhythm, one that combines the characteristics of both rhythms.

This work for two percussionists and a listening, invisibly conducting, computer is called *Duel*. In the mid-80s, I worked for many months, with a lot of passion and pleasure, on one of the first computers that was fast enough to work on these sorts of ideas.

The première took place in the summer of 1988 at the First International Symposium of Electronic Art in Utrecht, The Netherlands. *Duel* was performed only three times after that, one being at the International Computer Music Conference in Cologne, Germany.

After this compositional experiment, I struggled mainly with the question: Why didn't the computer always do what it was asked to do? Why did it sometimes fail to gauge the tempo correctly? Why did it hear a note as a crotchet, when it was just a slightly delayed quaver? These may seem to be simple problems, but if, for example, you try to explain to a computer what determines the tempo in a piece of music, then it soon becomes clear that it is you, rather than the computer, who lacks knowledge.

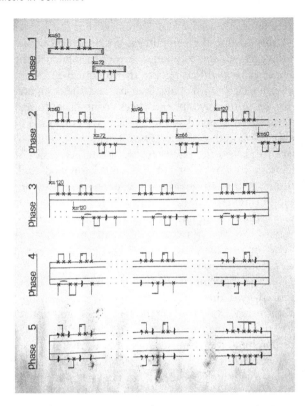

Figure 14.1 Score of *Duel for two percussionists*. Two percussionists start with playing a–free to choose–repetitive rhythm (top left) and are then, in five movements or phases, guided by a "conducting" computer towards playing exactly the same rhythm, one that combines the characteristics of both rhythms (bottom right) (Facsimile score provided by the author).

Working on *Duel* had far-reaching consequences for me personally. Up to that time, I had been mainly interested in the act of *making music*, combined with a fascination for the possibilities offered by the computer—a facility that had only just become available to everyone. After this same computer had rubbed my nose in the facts, I saw the limitations of my knowledge, and of music theory in general. And that gave me the motivation to try and gain a better understanding of the processes involved in *listening to music*. Finally, in 1997, that gave the impulse to start the Music, Mind, Machine project: an ambitious research project in which both the universities of Amsterdam and Nijmegen took part.

1998: A MECHANICAL SHOE

Ten years later, the internal parts of the listening computer looked very different! The machine could not do as much and was far from being the jack-of-all-trades that I needed for *Duel*. It could only produce the beat: an early attempt to incorporate beat induction into a computer model. The computer "listened" to a signal comparable to the one that we had fed into our first computer model. Using this information, this new model then calculated the expected beat derived from the music it got as input.

Because there is not much to see on a listening computer—no baton, no wild gestures—we engineered a mechanical shoe. When the computer anticipated the beat, then it lifted the shoe up early enough so that, exactly in time with the beat, it could let it drop again.

However, the new computer program failed to carry out the assignment without making mistakes. This time, that was exactly the intention! It had not been our aim to make the best machine in the world, one that was always able to find the correct solution,

Figure 14.2 A mechanical and anticipating beat-tapping shoe, connected to a "listening" computer.

just as a good percussionist might also have been able to do. No, I wanted a machine that moved its foot in the same way as the average listener; a shoe that, for example, in a very human, and therefore understandable way hesitates briefly if the tempo suddenly changes. Would it? Would it not?—*That* made it interesting.

At the same time, our research group organized a competition with a number of international colleagues between various computer models programmed for beat induction. Among those taking part were scientists from the US (Edward Large), England (Richard Parncutt), and Japan (Masataka Goto). Each computer model was given its own kind of shoe: the English team used a rubber rainboot, the Japanese a slipper, the North Americans a sneaker, and the Dutch, of course, a wooden shoe.

In the end, it turned out to be more a demonstration than a competition, because none of the models tapped as a real person would do. What did arise from this competition was the idea of following it up with a variation of the *Turing Test*. This is a test devised by the mathematician Alan Turing in the first half of the twentieth century to gauge to what extent a system demonstrates human intelligence.

For example, via a computer someone can communicate with one or more people and computers, without knowing with whom they are speaking. If, afterwards, this person is unsure which messages have come from people and which from a computer, then the computer would pass the Turing Test.

So far, that has turned out to be quite a challenge: most computer systems have been unmasked. However, all this becomes feasible if the rules are tightened up, as in the *Limited Turing Test*, where the domain is very restricted.

For beat induction we devised a variation of this test. We placed a series of computers and one person behind a curtain. Out of sight to participants who were listening to different fragments of music, the computers and the one person each operated their own mechanical shoe that moved up and down in front of the curtain. The task for a panel of experts was to identify which of the shoes had been operated by a human, rather than by a computer. The computer that was most frequently confused with a human foot-tapper would win the main prize.

Unfortunately, it has never been possible to carry out this test on a large scale, but my expectation is that even the present computer

Figure 14.3 The Limited Turing Test. Which shoe taps in the most human way to the beat of the music?

models that are programmed for beat induction would have a lot of difficulty in completing this test.

2008: TOWARDS A SCIENCE OF LISTENING

Just as with so many people, my fascination for music began early in life. As a teenager, I endlessly played gramophone records with my brothers in our attic; listening to where the "groove" was, and then moving the needle back a little, time and again. You could hear the "groove," but what was it exactly? Did it come just after the beat, or just before? Listening to what you heard, devising a theory, and then playing it yourself to achieve the same effect: there is hardly anything more exciting than that!

In fact, I do much the same in my current research, except that the computer has replaced the gramophone, and a personal judgment is put into perspective and objectified by large-scale listening experiments that make use of Internet.

Fortunately, however, the fun in listening, and trying to understand why something sounds exciting, sad, or awkward is still just as great. Together with a team of researchers, this gave the motivation, year after year, to try and understand "the secret of the loud rest" and "the secret of the details." Step-by-step, these were mysteries that we have now been able to unravel.

However, there is still much to be discovered about the origins and development of our capacity for music. *Musicality* has now become one of the core topics of my research. The research with newborns (see Chapter 7) was an initial step; it placed our earlier studies of beat induction, which were hitherto mainly musicological and computational in nature, in an entirely new perspective. It once again threw a spanner into my research agenda. Why were these newborns surprised by the omission of a beat in a varying rhythm? Were we observing an innate aptitude or at least a biological function active from day one? Is beat induction a music-specific, or even a human-specific trait? And could beat induction have played a founding role in the evolution of music?

2018: THE BIOLOGICAL BASIS OF MUSICALITY

While earlier studies have suggested that beat induction is learned, for example, by being rocked by one's parents to the beat of the music, recent research show this to be improbable; motion undoubtedly has an effect on the further development of metrical sensitivity, but the basic skill is clearly present directly after birth. It is remarkable that while most humans have little trouble tapping their foot to the beat of the music, or hearing whether music speeds up or slows down, it is still impossible to get species closely related to us, such as chimpanzees and other primates, to clap or drum to the beat of the music (see Chapter 7). They appear not to have a feeling for meter. Certain species of bird, however—parrots and cockatoos, for instance—do seem to be able to hear a beat, if we are to take the listening experiments with Snowball seriously.

How can the cognitive and biological building blocks of musicality, such as beat induction and relative pitch, be evaluated? What traits do we share with cockatoos and not with our nearest relatives such as chimpanzees or macaques?

If humans share beat induction with specific avian species and other "vocal learners" like dolphins and seals, then this makes the phenomenon even more intriguing, and its evolutionary implications all the more fascinating for researchers: which biological and/or social traits do we share with parrots, songbirds, and seals—but apparently not with other primates—and what does this tell us about the evolution of musicality?

The possible answers to these questions have been the subject of much discussion. Some researchers regard the study of the evolution of music cognition (and cognition in general) as well-nigh impossible, doomed to remain, at best, an engaging story. Other researchers devise strategies to judge whether it is indeed possible to support the cognitive and biological role of musicality.

Our Amsterdam research group has recently begun developing one such possible strategy. Its aim is to hone in on and precisely define the fundamental mechanisms, the building blocks, from which musicality appears to be constructed (such as beat induction and relative pitch) and subsequently to support this with empirical evidence drawn from various sources and disciplines.

In parallel, more and more researchers, from music psychology to neuroscience and computational musicology to bio-musicology, are contributing to an understanding of our capacity for music (see Honing, 2018 for an overview). Hence, I'm sure that, in the coming years, we can expect more and more scientifically supported insights into *what makes us musical animals*.

SUMMARY

By programming a computer to "listen" (making sense of the fundamental features of music) and to "conduct" (instruct musicians what to do next), we comprehend more and more of what we do and do not know about how music works in the human mind. The methodologies of the cognitive sciences come to real use here, recently extended with the toolkits of biology and the neurosciences. Music cognition has become a truly interdisciplinary field.

FURTHER READING

Honing, H. (Ed.) (2018). *The Origins of Musicality*. Cambridge, MA: The MIT Press.

Honing, H. (2019). *The Evolving Animal Orchestra. In Search of What Makes Us Musical.* Cambridge, MA: The MIT Press.

Huron, D. (2006). *Sweet Anticipation: Music and the Psychology of Expectation.* Cambridge, MA: The MIT Press.

Levitin, D. J. (2019). *This Is Your Brain on Music: Understanding a Human Obsession.* New York, NY: Penguin.

Margulis, E. H. (2014). *On Repeat: How Music Plays the Mind*. New York, NY: Oxford University Press.

Sacks, O. (2007). *Musicophilia: Tales of Music and the Brain*. New York, NY: Knopf.

Tan, S.-L., Pfordresher, P. Q., & Harré, R. (2010). *Psychology of Music: From Sound to Significance* (2nd edition). Abingdon: Routledge.

Thompson, W. F. (2015). *Music, Thought, and Feeling: Understanding the Psychology of Music*. Oxford: Oxford University Press.

BIBLIOGRAPHY

Adler, G. (1885). "Umfang, Methode und Ziel der Musikwissenschaft." *Vierteljahresschrift für Musikwissenschaft*, 1, 5–20.

Adorno, T. W. (1938). "On the fetish character in music and the regression of listening." In *The Essential Frankfurt School Reader*, Blackwell, (p. 280).

Ashley, R. (2002). "Do[n't] change a hair for me: The art of jazz rubato." *Music Perception*, 19 (3), 311–332.

Bååth, R., Lagerstedt, E., & Gärdenfors, P. (2013). "An oscillator model of categorical rhythm perception." In M. Knauff *et al.* (Eds.) *Proceedings of the 35th Annual Conference of the Cognitive Science Society* (pp. 1803–1808).

Bamberger, J. (1996). "Turning music theory on its ear." *International Journal of Computers for Mathematical Learning*, 1, 33–55.

Barenboim, D. (2006). "Lecture 2: The neglected sense," BBC Reith Lectures. London: BBC Radio.

Bellis, M. A. *et al.* (2007). "Elvis to Eminem: quantifying the price of fame through early mortality of European and North American rock and pop stars." *Journal of Epidemiology and Community Health*, 61, 896–901.

Bernstein, L. (1976). *The Unanswered Question*. Cambridge, MA: The MIT Press.

Bigand, E., D'Adamo, D. A., & Poulin-Charronnat, B. (2003). "The implicit learning of a contemporary musical grammar." In *Proceedings of the European Society for Cognitive Psychology*. Granada, Spain: Granada University.

Bigand, E. & Poulin-Charronnat, B. (2006). "Are we 'experienced listeners'? A review of the musical capacities that do not depend on formal musical training." *Cognition*, 100, 100–130.

Bod, R. (2002). "A unified model of structural organization in language and music." *Journal of Artificial Intelligence Research*, 17, 289–308.

Brochard, R., Abecasis, D., Potter, D., Ragot, R., & Drake, C. (2003). "The 'ticktock' of our internal clock: Direct brain evidence of subjective accents in isochronous sequences." *Psychological Science*, 14, 362–366.

Cage, J. (1952). *4'33": For Any Instrument or Combination of Instruments*. New York: Edition Peters.

Castellano, M. A., Bharucha, J. J., & Krumhansl, C. L. (1984). "Tonal hierarchies in the music of North India." *Journal of Experimental Psychology: General*, 113, 394–412.

Chomsky, N. (1965). *Aspects of the Theory of Syntax*. Cambridge, MA: The MIT Press.

Clarke, E. F. (1999). "Rhythm and timing in music." In D. Deutsch (Ed.), *Psychology of Music*, 2nd edition (pp. 473–500). New York: Academic Press.

Cook, P. F., Rouse, A., Wilson, M., & Reichmuth, C. (2013). "A California sea lion (Zalophus californianus) can keep the beat: Motor entrainment to rhythmic auditory stimuli in a non vocal mimic." *Journal of Comparative Psychology*, 127 (2), 412–427.

Cooke, D. (1959). *The Language of Music*. Oxford: Oxford University Press.

Coon, H. & Carey, G. (1989). "Genetic and environmental determinants of musical ability in twins," *Behavior Genetics*, 19, 183–193.

Cross, I. (2001). "Music, mind and evolution." *Psychology of Music*, 19, 95–102.

Cuddy, L. L., Balkwill, L. L., Peretz, I., & Holden, R. R. (2005). "Musical difficulties are rare: A study of 'tone deafness' among university students." *Annals of the New York Academy of Sciences*, 1060, 311–324.

Dalla Bella, S., Giguère, J-F., & Peretz, I. (2007). "Singing proficiency in the general population." *Journal of The Acoustical Society of America*, 121, 1182–1189.

Dalla Bella, S. & Peretz, I. (2005). "Differentiation of classical music requires little learning but rhythm." *Cognition*, 96, B65–B78.

Darwin, G. (1871). *The Descent of Man, and Selection in Relation to Sex*. London: Murray.

DeCaspar, A. J. & Fifer, W. P. (1980). "Of human bonding: newborns prefer their mothers' voice." *Science*, 208, 1174–1176.

Delaere, M. (2006). "De toekomst van de muziekwetenschap: Wat is een partituur?" [The future of musicology: What is a score?]. *Tijdschrift voor Muziektheorie*, 11, 31–35.

Desain, P. & Honing, H. (1989). "Quantization of musical time: A connectionist approach." *Computer Music Journal*, 13, 56–66.

Desain, P. & Honing, H. (1994). "Foot-tapping: A brief introduction to beat induction." In *Proceedings of the 1994 International Computer Music Conference* (pp. 78–79). San Francisco, CA: International Computer Music Association.

Desain, P. & Honing, H. (1995). "Computationeel modelleren van beat-inductie [The computational modelling of beat induction]." In *Van frictie tot wetenschap: Jaarboek 1994–1995* (pp. 83–95). Amsterdam: Vereniging van Academie-onderzoekers.

Desain, P. & Honing, H. (1999). "Computational models of beat induction: The rule-based approach." *Journal of New Music Research*, 28, 29–42.

Desain, P. & Honing, H. (2003). "The formation of rhythmic categories and metric priming." *Perception*, 32, 341–365.

Desain, P. & Honing, H. (2004). Final report NWO-PIONIER project "Music, Mind, Machine." *Technical Notes ILLC*, X-2004–2002. Amsterdam: Institute for Logic, Language and Computation, Universiteit van Amsterdam.

De Waal, F. B. M. & Ferrari, P. F. (2010). "Towards a bottom-up perspective on animal and human cognition." *Trends in Cognitive Sciences*, 14, 201–207.

Dienes, Z. & Longuet-Higgins, H. C. (2004). "Can musical transformations be implicitly learned?" *Cognitive Science*, 28, 531–558.

Dostoyevsky, F. M. (1866; 1999). *Crime and Punishment*. New York: Signet (p. 3).

Dowling, W. J. (1999). "Development of music perception and cognition." In D. Deutsch (Ed.), *The Psychology of Music* (pp. 603–625), 2nd edition. New York: Academic Press.

Drake, C. (1997). "Motor and perceptually preferred synchronisation by children and adults: Binary and ternary ratios." *Polish Quarterly of Developmental Psychology*, 3, 41–59.

Fernald, A. (1989). "Intonation and communicative intent in mothers' speech to infants: is the melody the message?" *Child Development*, 60, 1497–1510.

Fitch, W. T. (2006). "The biology and evolution of music: a comparative perspective." *Cognition*, 100, 173.

Fodor, J. A. (1983). *The Modularity of Mind: An Essay in Faculty Psychology*. Cambridge, MA: MIT Press.

Fraisse, P. (1982). "Rhythm and tempo." In D. Deutsch (Ed.), *Psychology of Music* (pp. 149–180). New York: Academic Press.

Francès, R. (1958). *La perception de la musique [The perception of music]*. Paris: Librairie Philosophique J. Vrin.

Gann, K. (2010). *No Such Thing As Silence: John Cage's 4'33"*. New Haven: Yale University Press.

Gjerdingen, R.O. & Perrott, D. (2008). "Scanning the dial: The rapid recognition of music genres." *Journal of New Music Research*, 37, 93–100.

Gould, S. J. & Vrba, E. S. (1982). "Exaptation—a missing term in the science of form." *Paleobiology*, 8, 4–15.

Grahn, J. (2009). "Neuroscientific investigations of musical rhythm: Recent advances and future challenges." *Contemporary Music Review*, 28, 251–277.

Groot, G. (20 January2006). "Leesluisteren is onvergeeflijk," *NRC Handelsblad, Cultureel Supplement*.

Grove Music Online (2009). Entry "Syncopation." See www.oxford musi conline.com/subscriber/article/grove/music/27263.

Haanstra, B. (1987). Een monument voor een gorilla [Monument for a gorilla]. Bert Haanstra Films.

Hannon, E. E. & Trehub, S. E. (2005). "Metrical categories in infancy and adulthood." *Psychological Science*, 16, 48–55.

Hannon, E. E. & Trehub, S. E. (2005). "Tuning in to musical rhythms: Infants learn more readily than adults." *Proceedings of the National Academy of Sciences*, 102, 12639–12643.

Harnad, S. (Ed.) (1987). *Categorical Perception: The Groundwork of Cognition*. New York: Cambridge University Press.

Von Helmholtz, H. (1863; 1954). *On the Sensations of Tone as a Physiological Basis for the Theory of Music*. New York: Dover Publications.

Honing, H. (2001). "From time to time: The representation of timing and tempo." *Computer Music Journal*, 35, 50–61.

Honing, H. (2003). "The final ritard: On music, motion, and kinematic models." *Computer Music Journal*, 27, 66–72.

Honing, H. (2006). "Evidence for tempo-specific timing in music using a web-based experimental setup." *Journal of Experimental Psychology: Human Perception and Performance*, 32, 780–786.

Honing, H. (2006). "On the growing role of observation, formalization and experimental method in musicology." *Empirical Musicological Review*, 1, 2–5.

Honing, H. (2006). "Computational modeling of music cognition: A case study on model selection." *Music Perception*, 23, 365–376.

Honing, H. (2007). "Is expressive timing relational invariant under tempo transformation?" *Psychology of Music*, 35, 276–285.

Honing, H. (2011). *The Illiterate Listener. On Music Cognition, Musicality and Methodology*. Amsterdam: Amsterdam University Press.

Honing, H. (2012). "Without it no music: beat induction as a fundamental musical trait." *Annals of the New York Academy of Sciences*, 1252 (1), 85–91.

Honing, H. (2013). "Structure and interpretation of rhythm in music." In D. Deutsch (Ed.), *Psychology of Music*, 3rd edition (pp. 369–404). London, UK: Academic Press.

Honing, H. (2018). "On the biological basis of musicality." *Annals of the New York Academy of Sciences*, 1423 (1), 51–56.

Honing, H. & de Haas, W. B. (2008). "Swing once more: Relating timing and tempo in expert jazz drumming." *Music Perception*, 25 (5), 471–476.

Honing, H. & Ladinig, O. (2009). "Exposure influences expressive timing judgments in music." *Journal of Experimental Psychology: Human Perception and Performance*, 35, 281–288.

Honing, H. & Ploeger, A. (2012). "Cognition and the evolution of music: Pitfalls and prospects." *Topics in Cognitive Science*, 4, 513–524.

Van den Hout, F. (2008). Het muzikale brein [The musical brain]. *Psychologie Magazine*, 27, 30–33.

Huron, D. (1999). "The new empiricism: systematic musicology in a post-modern age. The 1999 Ernest Bloch Lectures." [online only] Berkeley, CA: University of California.

Huron, D. (2003). "Is music an evolutionary adaptation?" In Wallin, N. L., Merker, B., & Brown, S. (Eds.) *The Origins of Music* (pp. 57–75). Cambridge, MA: The MIT Press.

Huron, D. (2008). *Sweet Anticipation: Music and the Psychology of Expectation.* Cambridge, MA: The MIT Press, (p. 200).

Jackendoff, R. (2002). *Foundations of Language.* New York: Oxford University Press.

Jacoby, N. & McDermott, J. H. (2017). "Integer ratio priors on musical rhythm revealed cross-culturally by iterated reproduction." *Current Biology,* 27, 359–370.

Kalmus, H. & Fry, D. B. (1980). "On tune deafness (dysmelodia): Frequency, development, genetics and musical background." *Annals of Human Genetics,* 43, 369–382.

Kass, J. H., Hackett, T. A., & Tramo, M. J. (1999). "Auditory processing in primate cerebral cortex." *Current Opinion in Neurobiology,* 9, 164–170.

Kessler, E. J., Hansen, C., & Shepard, R. N. (1984). "Tonal schemata in the perception of music in Bali and in the West." *Music Perception,* 2, 131–166.

Kostelanetz, R. (1988). *Conversing with Cage.* New York: Limelight Editions (p. 189).

Kramer, J. (2007). *Why Classical Music Still Matters,* Berkley, CA: University of California Press.

Krumhansl, C. L. (1990). *Cognitive Foundations of Musical Pitch.* New York: Oxford University Press.

Krumhansl, C. L. (2000). "Rhythm and pitch in music cognition." *Psychological Bulletin,* 126, 159–179.

Ladinig, O. & Honing, H. (2008). "An empirically validated model of complexity: Longuet-Higgins and Lee reconsidered." In *Proceedings of the International Conference on Music Perception and Cognition* (p. 123). Sapporo, Japan: Hokkaido University.

Ladinig, O., Honing, H., Háden, G., & Winkler, I. (2009). "Probing attentive and pre-attentive emergent meter in adult listeners with no extensive music training." *Music Perception,* 26, 377–386.

Large, E. W. & Gray, P. M. (2015). "Spontaneous tempo and rhythmic entrainment in a bonobo (Pan paniscus)." *Journal of Comparative Psychology,* 129 (4), 317–328.

Large, E. W. & Jones, M. R. (1999). "The dynamics of attending: How people track time- varying events." *Psychological Review,* 106 (1), 119–159.

Lerdahl, F. (1992). "Cognitive constraints on compositional systems." *Contemporary Music Review,* 6, 97–121.

Lerdahl, F. & Jackendoff, R. (1983). *A Generative Theory of Tonal Music*. Cambridge, MA: The MIT Press.

Levitin, D. J. (1994). "Absolute memory for musical pitch: Evidence from the production of learned melodies." *Perception & Psychophysics*, 56, 414–423.

Lewontin, R. C. (1998). "The evolution of cognition: Questions we will never answer." In D. Scarborough & S. Sternberg (Eds.) *Methods, Models, and Conceptual Issues: An Invitation to Cognitive Science*, Vol. 4 (pp. 107–132). Cambridge, MA: MIT Press.

London, J. M. (1993). "Loud rests and other strange metric phenomena (or, meter as heard)." *Music Theory Online*, 0 (2).

Longuet-Higgins, H. C. (1994). "Artificial intelligence and musical cognition." *Philosophical Transactions Royal Society London*, A (349), 103–113.

Longuet-Higgins, H. C. & Lee, C. S. (1984). "The rhythmic interpretation of monophonic music." *Music Perception*, 1, 424–441.

Loy, G. (2006). *Musimathics: The Mathematical Foundations of Music*. Cambridge, MA: The MIT Press.

Lynch, M. P., Eilers, R. E., Oller, D. K., & Urbano, R. C. (1990). "Innateness, experience and music perception." *Psychological Science*, 1, 272–276.

MacDougall, H. G. & Moore, S. T. (2005). "Marching to the beat of the same drummer: The spontaneous tempo of human locomotion." *Journal of Applied Physiology*, 99, 1164–1173.

Mampe, B., Friederici, A. D., Christophe, A., & Wermke, K. (2009). "Newborns' cry melody is shaped by their native language." *Current Biology*, 19 (23), 1994–1997.

Margulis, E. H. (2019). *The Psychology of Music: A Very Short Introduction*. Oxford, UK: Oxford University Press.

Marmel, F., Tillmann, B., & Dowling, W. J. (2008). "Tonal expectations influence pitch perception." *Perception & Psychophysics*, 70, 841–852.

Martin, J. G. (1972). "Rhythmic (hierarchic) versus serial structure in speech and other behaviour." *Psychological Review*, 79, 487–509.

Martínez-Molina, N., Mas-Herrero, E., Rodríguez-Fornells, A., Zatorre, R. J., & Marco-Pallarés, J. (2016). "Neural correlates of specific musical anhedonia." *Proceedings of the National Academy of Sciences*, 113 (46), E7337–E7345.

Masharov, M. & Fischer, M. (2006). "Linguistic relativity: does language help or hinder perception?" *Current Biology*, 16, R289–R291.

Matlock, D.*et al.* (2008). "'Stayin' Alive': A pilot study to test the effectiveness of a novel mental metronome in maintaining appropriate compression rates in simulated cardiac arrest scenarios." *Annals of Emergency Medicine*, 52, S67–S68.

Mattys, S. L., Jusczyk, P. W., Luce, P. A., & Morgan, J. L. (1999). "Phonotactic and prosodic effects on word segmentation in infants." *Cognitive Psychology*, 38, 465–494.

McDonald, C. & Stewart, L. (2008). "Uses and functions of music in congenital amusia." *Music Perception*, 25, 345–355.

Mehr, S., Krasnow, M., Bryant, G., & Hagen, E. (2020). "Origins of music in credible signaling." *Behavioral and Brain Sciences*, 1–41.

Merchant, H. & Honing, H. (2014). "Are non-human primates capable of rhythmic entrainment? Evidence for the gradual audiomotor evolution hypothesis." *Frontiers in Auditory Cognitive Neuroscience*, 7 (274), 1–8.

Miller, G. F. (2000). "Evolution of human music through sexual selection." In Wallin, N. L., Merker, B., & Brown, S. (Eds.) *The Origins of Music* (pp. 329–360). Cambridge, MA: The MIT Press.

Miller, G. F. (2001). *The Mating Mind: How Sexual Choice Shaped the Evolution of Human Nature*. London: Vintage.

Miyazaki, K. (1988). "Musical pitch identification by absolute pitch possessors." *Perception & Psychophysics*, 44, 501–512.

Miyazaki, K. (1993). "Absolute pitch as an inability: Identification of musical intervals in a tonal context." *Music Perception*, 11, 55–72.

Partch, H. (1979). *Genesis of a Music*. New York: Da Capo Press.

Patel, A. (2008). *Music, Language, and the Brain*. Oxford: Oxford University Press (pp. 283–297).

Patel, A. D. & Iversen, J. R. (2006). "A non-human animal can drum a steady beat on a musical instrument." In *Proceedings of the International Conference on Music Perception and Cognition* (p. 477). Bologna, Italy: University of Bologna.

Patel, A. D., Iversen, J. R., Bregman, M. R., & Schulz, I. (2009). "Experimental evidence for synchronization to a musical beat in a nonhuman animal." *Current Biology*, 19, 827–830.

Peretz, I. & Coltheart, M. (2003). "Modularity of music processing." *Nature Neuroscience*, 6, 688–691.

Peretz, I. & Hyde, K. (2003). "What is specific to music processing? Insights from congenital amusia." *Trends in Cognitive Sciences*, 7, 362–367.

Phillips-Silver, J. & Trainor, L. J. (2005). "Feeling the beat: Movement influences infants' rhythm perception." *Science*, 308, 1430.

Pinker, S. (1997). *How the Mind Works*. New York: W. W. Norton & Company (p. 532).

Rauscher, F. H., Shaw, G. L., & Ky, K. N. (1993). "Music and spatial task performance." *Nature*, 365, 611.

Réale, D.*et al.* (2009). "Male personality, life-history strategies and reproductive success in a promiscuous mammal." *Journal of Evolutionary Biology*, 22, 1599–1607.

Révész, G. (1913). *Zur Grundlegung der Tonpsychologie*. Leipzig, Germany: Veit.

Ross, A. (2007). *The Rest is Noise: Listening to the Twentieth Century*. New York: Farrar, Strauss and Giroux, p. 524.

Sacks, O. (2007). *Musicophilia: Tales of Music and the Brain*. New York: Knopf.

Sadakata, M., Weidema, J. L., & Honing, H. (2020). "Parallel pitch processing in speech and melody: A study of the interference of musical melody on lexical pitch perception in speakers of Mandarin." *PLOS One*, 15 (3), 1–14.

Saffran, J. R. (2003). "Absolute pitch in infancy and adulthood: The role of tonal structure." *Developmental Science*, 6, 37–45.

Saffran, J. R., & Griepentrog, G. J. (2001). "Absolute pitch in infant auditory learning: evidence for developmental reorganization." *Developmental Psychology*, 37, 74–85.

Savage, P., Loui, P., Tarr, B., Schachner, A., Glowacki, L., Mithen, S., & Fitch, W. (2020). "Music as a coevolved system for social bonding." *Behavioral and Brain Sciences*, 1–36.

Savenije, W. (12 December2005). "Brautigam is top in Beethoven," *NRC Handelsblad*.

Schachner, A., Brady, T., Pepperberg, I., & Hauser, M. (2009). "Spontaneous motor entrainment to music in multiple vocal mimicking species." *Current Biology*, 19, 831–836.

Schellenberg, E. G. & Trehub, S. E. (2003). "Good pitch memory is widespread." *Psychological Science*, 14, 262–266.

Schönberger, E. (2005). *Het gebroken oor* [*The Broken Ear*]. Amsterdam: Meulenhoff.

Seger, C. A. (1994). "Implicit learning." *Psychological Bulletin*, 115, 163–196.

Serafine, M. L. (1988). *Music as Cognition: The Development of Thought in Sound*. New York: Columbia University Press.

Sloboda, J. A., Wise, K. J. & Peretz, I. (2005). "Quantifying tone deafness in the general population." *Annals of the New York Academy of Sciences*, 1060, 255–261.

Smith, L. M. & Honing, H. (2006). "Evaluating and extending computational models of rhythmic syncopation in music." In *Proceedings of the International Computer Music Conference* (pp. 688–691). San Francisco, CA: International Computer Music Association.

Takeuchi, A. H. & Hulse, S. H. (1991). "Absolute-pitch judgments of black- and white-key pitches." *Music Perception*, 9, 27–46.

Takeuchi, A. H. & Hulse, S. H. (1993). "Absolute pitch." *Psychological Bulletin*, 113, 345–361.

Thompson, W.F., Schellenberg, G. E., & Husain, G. (2001). "Arousal, mood, and the Mozart effect." *Psychological Science*, 12, 248–251.

Todd, N. P. M, Cousins, R. & Lee, C. S. (2007). "The contribution of anthropometric factors to individual differences in the perception of rhythm." *Empirical Musicology Review*, 2, 1–13.

Tomasello, M. (2008). *Origins of Human Communication*. Cambridge, MA: The MIT Press.

Trainor, L. J. (2007). "Do preferred beat rate and entrainment to the beat have a common origin in movement?" *Empirical Musicology Review*, 2, 17–20.

Trainor, L. J., Austin, C. M., & Desjardins, R. N. (2000). "Is infant-directed speech prosody a result of the vocal expression of emotion?" *Psychological Science*, 11, 188–195.

Trainor, L. J. & Trehub, S. E. (1992). "A comparison of infants' and adults' sensitivity to Western musical structure." *Journal of Experimental Psychology: Human Perception and Performance*, 18, 394–402.

Trehub, S. E. (2003). "The developmental origins of musicality." *Nature Neuroscience*, 6, 669–673.

Trehub, S. E. & Hannon, E. E. (2006). "Infant music perception: Domain general or domain-specific mechanisms?" *Cognition*, 100, 73–98.

Trevarthen, C. (1979). "Communication and co-operation in early infancy: a description of primary intersubjectivity." In M. Bullowa (Ed.) *Before Speech: The Beginnings of Human Communication.* London: Cambridge University Press.

Turing, A. M. (1950). "Computing machinery and intelligence." *Mind*, 59, 433–460.

Vitouch, O. (2003). "Absolutist models of absolute pitch are absolutely misleading." *Music Perception*, 21, 111–117.

Vitouch, O., & Ladinig, O. (Eds.) (2009). "Music and evolution." *Musicae Scientiae, Special Issue*, 2009–2010.

Werker, J. F. & Tees, R. C (1999). "Influences on infant speech processing." *Annual Review of Psychology*, 50, 509–535.

Wright, A. A., Rivera, J. J., Hulse, S. H., Shyan, M., & Neiworth, J. J. (2000). "Music perception and octave generalization in rhesus monkeys." *Journal of Experimental Psychology: General*, 129, 291–307.

Yin, P., Fritz, J.B., Shihab A., & Shamma, S. A. (2010). "Do ferrets perceive relative pitch?" *Journal of the Acoustical Society of America*, 127, 1673–1680.

Zarco, W., Merchant, H., Prado, L., & Mendez, J. C. (2009). "Subsecond timing in primates: comparison of interval production between human subjects and rhesus monkeys." *Journal of Neurophysiology*, 102, 3191–3202.

Zentner, M. R., & Eerola, T. (2010). "Rhythmic engagement with music in infancy." *Proceedings of the National Academy of Sciences*, 107, 5768–5773.

Zentner, M. R. & Kagan, J. (1996). "Perception of music by infants." *Nature*, 383, 29.

INDEX

Printed in the United States
by Baker & Taylor Publisher Services